IMAGES
of America

KNOXVILLE IN THE CIVIL WAR

Gay Street, Knoxville, April 1861. As a vote on Tennessee's future in the Union approached, US senator Andrew Johnson spoke openly against a pending secessionist convention. While he commanded the attention of a crowd in front of the Lamar House hotel, a Confederate regimental band marched down the street, disrupting the gathering. Violence was barely averted by the intervention of several pro-Confederate civilians. (Courtesy of Richard E. Williams.)

On the Cover: **Orlando Poe and Orville Babcock on the Battlefield at Fort Sanders.** In March 1864, engineers Poe (left) and Babcock revisited the site of the disastrous Confederate assault made on November 29, 1863. The stumps used to construct an innovative telegraph wire entanglement are clearly visible. Army photographer George Barnard accompanied Captain Poe from Nashville through Chattanooga to document the Knoxville Campaign. (Library of Congress.)

IMAGES
of America

KNOXVILLE IN THE CIVIL WAR

Joan L. Markel, PhD

ARCADIA PUBLISHING

ISBN 978-1-4671-1019-8

Published by Arcadia Publishing
Charleston, South Carolina

Printed in the United States of America

Library of Congress Control Number: 2013930895

For all general information, please contact Arcadia Publishing:
Telephone 843-853-2070
Fax 843-853-0044
E-mail sales@arcadiapublishing.com
For customer service and orders:
Toll-Free 1-888-313-2665

Visit us on the Internet at www.arcadiapublishing.com

To Evan and Andrea

Contents

Acknowledgments 6

Introduction 7

1. The Battle of Fort Sanders 9
2. Fortification 23
3. Getting to Knoxville 39
4. Confederate Occupation 53
5. Federal Occupation 69
6. Knoxville, a Proud City 83
7. Families 97
8. Memory 113

ACKNOWLEDGMENTS

Since coming to East Tennessee over 20 years ago, I have gained an appreciation for this unique place and its culture. Growing up in the Northeast, going to college in the Midwest, and residing in California for many years, I thought I was ready for my Southern experience. Living among the good people of East Tennessee, I have slowly learned subtle conventions that eluded me in the beginning. It has taken me some time to appreciate the fact that what is not said can be just as powerful as what is.

To the many east Tennesseans who have shared their family stories, you humanize the facts and dates of the history of this place. To all the folks from here and "not from here," you create our present-day culture. Coming together to rediscover the past of this beautiful part of the world we all now call home contributes value to our community. The past continues in the present, even when it has been silenced. Thanks go to all of y'all for your generous direct and indirect contributions to the production of this book. I am grateful for the following contributors: Jefferson Chapman, Steve and Nancy Dean, Jim and Lindsey McDonough, John Burkhart, Laura Powers, Bud Albers, Debbie Woodiel, Arlene Lynsky, Paul Tanguay, Tammie and Brian Burroughs, Jim Lyle, Bill Lawhon, George Lane, Earl and Pratibha Hess, Dennis Urban, Aaron Astor, Joe Spence, Gerald and Sandra Augustus, Mike Angst, Calvin Chappelle, Will Haslam, Susan Swan, Stephanie Drumheller-Horton, Eric Wayland, Lynne Sullivan, Mike Brown, Charles Reeves, Jim Tumblin, Larry Markel, Dot Kelly, Bob Young, Mark Kline, Maggie Johnson, Elizabeth Keller DeCorse, Bob Pennington, Lindsey Kromer, Alix Dempster, Jerry Cross, and Dewey Beard.

Special thanks to John Burkhart and Debbie Woodiel for their careful attention to detail.

KEY TO FREQUENTLY SEEN COURTESY LINES

AC	Author's collection
MHC	McClung Historical Collection, Knox County Library
MM	McClung Museum of Natural History and Culture, University of Tennessee
LC	Library of Congress
SPCL	University of Tennessee Libraries, Knoxville, Special Collections

Introduction

Knoxville has always been the heart of the mountain and valley culture of upper East Tennessee. From its earliest settlement as a frontier outpost through its rise to a major manufacturing and distribution center, the development of this ever-changing American city has been influenced by and contributed to that larger national saga. By examining the ways in which historical trends were embraced, rejected, or sometimes ignored by this regionally distinct but fluid cross section of the American population, it is easier to understand some of those very complex events. Observing how events played out in this "Switzerland of America" and how the lives of individuals were forever altered during the Civil War can be illuminating.

Since its founding in 1792, geography has been a dominating factor in the development of Knoxville. The inland water system through the valleys provided transport in this mountainous region, functioning as the highways of these early times. As river trade increased in scale, water-transport ventures were tried, but navigation of the Tennessee River could only be counted on during the wet seasons; profitable enterprises could not be sustained. Politics in the mid-19th century focused on improving the transportation options connecting Knoxville to the markets all around, thus promoting the growth of its wealth and status. It was not until the completion of the railroad in 1858 that the vast potential of trade with the Northeast and the greater South could be capitalized upon. When the war began, local merchants were prospering, creating business relationships, particularly with markets in the South and West. In fact, this establishment of trading relationships with markets in the South helped determine the loyalties of many of Knoxville's first families.

When the war began, the sons and grandsons of Knoxville's founding fathers were the political and economic leaders of a growing and surprisingly transient population, and because of the nature of any small, original frontier population, most of the core of community leaders and their families were blood relations. Robert Tracy McKenzie, in his excellent 2006 study *Lincolnites and Rebels*, finds that in 1860 five percent of the population possessed 66 percent of the wealth, which meant the control of much of the economy was in the hands of a few descendants of the earliest arrivals. Those who had moved west in the first half of the 19th century, often leaving families already established in other states, to find opportunities on the developing frontier also achieved success. About 10 percent of the city's population was African American; approximately, half were slaves in domestic service and the others free, with 28 percent of the free African American population owning property.

By 1860, many fine homes, impressive public buildings, and a growing economy defined the city of Knoxville. Progress and opportunity were real and thus threatened by the unsettled political situation at the national level. Local politicians were Whigs and Democrats, already fierce rivals, and the presidential election of 1860 was hotly debated in the city. Well-known local activists, such as Whig Parson William Brownlow and Democrat Dr. J.G.M. Ramsey, found themselves in opposition on almost every issue, including the overarching issue of secession. That animosity played out in the press and on the streets of Knoxville prior to and during the four years of war.

While the main cause of the Civil War was most certainly the institution of slavery, it did not play a major role as a justification for war in East Tennessee. Feeling no great affinity with the wealthy plantation owners of the Deep South, most East Tennessee Unionist leaders were nevertheless pro-slavery and held small numbers of slaves. They believed that the peculiar institution was best protected under the Constitution as written, and local politicians made multiple stump speeches in 1861 trying to explain this position to the rural population. Most people saw slavery as a "natural" institution strictly driven by social convention and not moral contemplation. In fact, many of the churches, ministers, and congregations were pro-slavery and supported the Confederacy. As a source of wealth, East Tennessee had little reason to own large worker groups, as the terrain and climate could not support profitable farms extensive enough to require slave labor. Despite earlier antislavery activities, this region, in the years immediately before the war, did not exhibit any significant abolitionist sentiment.

When the nation went to war, so did East Tennessee. Despite a serious legal effort by Unionists meeting in Knoxville and Greeneville in the spring of 1861 to secede from the State of Tennessee, geography again played a major factor making separation impossible. Bordered by Confederate states and the Cumberland Mountains along the Kentucky border, East Tennessee was cut off from the immediate arrival and protection of a Federal army. The last state to enter the Confederacy, Tennessee had nevertheless been prepared for war by a pro-Confederate governor. Troops were in Knoxville even as the final vote for disunion was taken, and these men from elsewhere in the South were allowed to participate in the city referendum. Except for the inclusion of those troops occupying Knoxville, the vote was almost evenly divided for and against joining the Confederacy.

Confederate troops were necessary to keep the Unionists peaceful and to ensure that the Confederate States Army (CSA), especially the eastern theater around Richmond and Washington, was supplied with manpower, provisions, and transport along the vitally important East Tennessee and Georgia and East Tennessee and Virginia Railroads. In general, these imported troops reflected the Richmond government's distrust of the area and looked at the civilian population as disloyal no matter what their avowed stance, producing an adversarial relationship with residents. Food shortages, disease, destruction of property, and depletion of civic resources descended upon the town. In the more rural counties, periodic military raids from Kentucky and Virginia, as well as armed partisan violence from bands supporting one side or the other, threatened the people left behind when men of fighting age left to join the Confederate army or the Union army.

Halfway through the war, as the military focus shifted to Chattanooga, the army of Gen. Ambrose Burnside took the recently evacuated and undefended city of Knoxville without a fight, and Federal troops occupied the place until the end of the war. These troops initially found the pro-Unionists to be welcoming and supportive, but as the occupation progressed, difficulties in establishing steady supply lines produced hungry troops who did not always distinguish between sympathies in the local population as they foraged for what they needed to survive. The strains of a major Confederate attack, the emphasis of military efforts elsewhere, the periodic military raids from Virginia, and the bushwhacker lawlessness by partisans of both sides left East Tennessee in a state of violence, material want, fear, and deprivation that lasted throughout the rest of the war.

The military history of East Tennessee is its own fascinating mixture of famous generals, brilliantly engineered fortifications, a clash of former rivals, and the presence of troops from all Southern and nearly all Northern states during the course of four years of war. From the first days of the war, Knoxville found itself occupied, housing and feeding thousands of nonproductive individuals. The horrible slaughter of some of the best troops of the Confederacy in November 1863 was an extreme instance of marching men into modern shells and bullets in enough number to overwhelm firepower with bodies. The outstanding performance and ultimate survival of the Union position achieved by superlative engineering efforts transformed Knoxville into "the keep of East Tennessee" for the rest of the war.

How that war played out militarily, how the people divided, how men of honor handled personal commitment while facing real danger—not just for themselves but for their families—how opportunists seeking personal gain supported whichever side was in control, how women managed a hostile home front, how divided families functioned in the midst of social chaos, and how that chaos has still not been totally resolved 150 years and five generations later will be covered in *Knoxville in the Civil War.* Knoxville's Civil War story is as much about the civilian population and its war within as it is about armies and battles.

One

The Battle of Fort Sanders

At first light on the morning of November 29, 1863, a bloody battle took place on a frozen hilltop west of Knoxville, Tennessee. From the protected position near the railroad tracks at the base of the hill, 4,000 seasoned Confederates massed to storm the fort at the summit. Inside the fortifications, initially some 220, soon reinforced to about 400, equally experienced Union defenders braced for the long-expected assault.

Gen. James Longstreet picked his attack point well. Natural geography made it possible for thousands of troops to mass close enough to overcome the firepower of the fort's artillery by direct assault. It was a simple matter of throwing enough bodies into lead projectiles to overwhelm the firing, and then hand-to-hand combat by superior numbers would secure the breech of the defenses. Many of the advancing soldiers did not even bother to load their rifles. Bayonets, knives, and side arms were the anticipated weapons of victory. By storming and taking this one point, the whole of the defenses of the town would fall.

A Confederate artillery barrage preceded the order to advance. As the troops began their "hep, hep, hep" up the hill, almost immediately a maze of nearly invisible telegraph wire strung from stump to stump tripped and disoriented the first ranks. Despite the confusion, most of the soldiers advanced only to encounter the ditch surrounding the northwest bastion of the fort. There was little choice but to descend into this death trap, some 12 to 20 feet wide, beneath the parapet overhead. They had neither tools to cut handholds in the icy, frozen red dirt wall or any scaling ladders. Some tried bayonets, and officers used their swords. A few made it to the top of the wall only to be shot, clubbed, or blown to pieces. Hotchkiss shells with paper fuses were thrown over the wall into the ditch. Blood was ankle deep as the dead, dying, and wounded fell entangled in a mass of human destruction. The slaughter was over in 20 minutes. "I know of no instance in history when the assaulting forces were so completely annihilated," wrote Orlando Poe, a Union engineer. The final outcome counted 813 casualties for the Confederates and 13 for the Federals.

"THE BATTLE OF FORT SANDERS" BY GREG HARLIN. At dawn on a cold, foggy morning, 4,000 battle-hardened veterans of CSA general Lafayette McLaws's division attacked the northwest bastion of the newly strengthened earthen fort. Badly clothed and many without shoes, these veterans of Fredericksburg, Gettysburg, and Chickamauga were stopped in only 20 minutes of unspeakable carnage. News of Bragg's defeat in Chattanooga precluded a second attempt to storm the heights. (MM)

"THE BATTLE OF FORT SANDERS" BY THOMAS NAST IN *HARPER'S WEEKLY*. Although the famous cartoonist was not in Knoxville, he thoroughly researched the events of the battle. Details include a Confederate officer in front of a cannon, the shooting of a soldier scaling the parapet, and the hurling of shells, which are incorrectly shown as spherical, into the ditch. For dramatic effect, Federals are shown standing on the parapet; Confederate sharpshooters would not have allowed that. (AC)

"The Battle of Fort Sanders" by Theodore Davis for *Harper's Weekly*. Like Nast, Davis did not seem to have been an eyewitness to the battle but he also included details of documented events of the action. Defenders inside the fort reported the clubbing of an attacker with the butt of a rifle, the throwing of short-fuse artillery shells into the ditch, and the attacking of soldiers with bayonets. (AC)

"The Battle of Fort Sanders," a Lithograph by Lloyd Branson. Knoxville artist Lloyd Branson created his interpretation of the battle for inclusion in Thomas Humes's 1888 book *The Loyal Mountaineers of East Tennessee*. In this sophisticated rendering, the details of terrain, fort construction, and a larger field of action give the impression of a full-scale battle. (AC)

"The Battle of Fort Sanders." In this less sophisticated depiction of the battle, the whole center group of soldiers is shown in full retreat, which was probably fairly accurate. Stumps and wire are clearly visible as well as a substantial berm, a reinforcing "shelf" at the base of the wall inside the trench. The soldiers here are more cartoonish than in the previous examples, but the terrain and formation are well done. (AC)

"Battle of Fort Sanders" from *Harper's Weekly.* Focusing on the CSA troops charging the bastion, this unattributed lithograph emphasizes the distribution of the soldiers and the larger formation of the attack. Details include hand-to-hand combat on the parapet and the university buildings in the upper right. Another earthen fort appears on a hilltop, possibly across the river, on the far right. (AC)

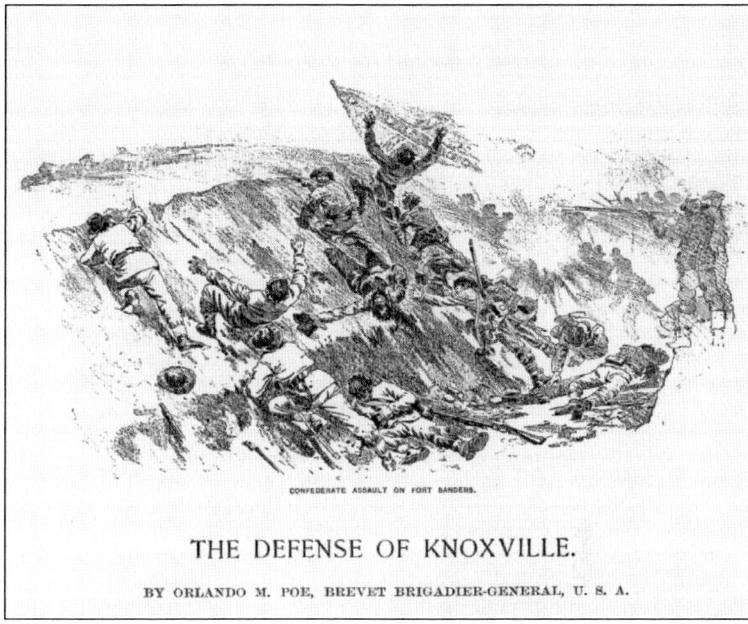

CONFEDERATE ASSAULT ON FORT SANDERS.

THE DEFENSE OF KNOXVILLE.

BY ORLANDO M. POE, BREVET BRIGADIER-GENERAL, U. S. A.

"The Battle of Fort Sanders" from *Battles and Leaders*. This image accompanied Orlando Poe's article, "Defense of Knoxville." It correctly shows that the berm cut away, and the Federals hunkered down behind the parapet. The shooting of a Confederate battle flag carrier on the parapet is also accurate. The Federals took a total of three battle flags during the attack. (AC)

"The Battle of Fort Sanders," a Kurtz and Allison Print. By the 1890s, the war was being romanticized by these popular printmakers from Chicago. In this version of the battle, Confederate troops have gold sashes, plumes in their hats, brand-new uniforms, and shiny black boots, and the ditch is filled with water like a castle moat. (AC)

***The Battle of Fort Sanders* by Knoxville Artist Russell Briscoe.** In this version of the battle, more attention is given to individual Confederate casualties and the view from the base of the hill. The original painting is in color, which helps to delineate the details of the rock, vegetation, and artillery craters through which the attack was made. (Courtesy of the East Tennessee Historical Society.)

***At First Light* by Ken Smith.** This is the only rendering of the battle of Fort Sanders from the perspective of the Confederate artillery positioned on Kingston Road to the west. Artillerist E. Porter Alexander conducted a withering barrage against the fort and the Union battery housed in the university buildings called Fort Byington. This site was archaeologically excavated in 2010. (MM)

Photograph of the Northwest Bastion. In March 1864, the details of the battlefield were captured in the fine photographic renderings performed by George Barnard. Orlando Poe returned to Knoxville to document the fortification of the town. This image shows the trench in great detail. Enlargements bring details of litter, probably left over from the battle, into focus. (LC)

738 *THE DEFENSE OF KNOXVILLE.*

THE NORTH-WESTERN BASTION OF FORT SANDERS, VIEWED FROM THE NORTH. FROM A WAR-TIME PHOTOGRAPH.

The Northwest Bastion from *Battles and Leaders*. Even 30 years after the war, in the 1890s, the technology did not exist for reproducing photographs in printed publications. The lithographers working for *Century Publications*, just as the lithographers of *Harper's Weekly* had done during the war, did an excellent job converting details of photographs into the printable lithographs needed for popular media. (AC)

The Ditch and Planks at Fort Sanders. In this Barnard photograph, details of the ditch are evident. Both Longstreet and E. Porter Alexander underestimated the depth of it; they did not realize that the men and dogs they had observed crossing were actually walking on planks. With better reconnaissance of the obstacle and more available resources, the attackers would have been issued scaling ladders and digging tools. (LC)

The Ditch at Fort Sanders, Looking North. This excellent photograph from the Library of Congress was long misidentified as Fort McAllister, Georgia, and attributed to another photographer. It is actually by Barnard and shows the ditch and northwest bastion taken from a position on the southwest bastion of Fort Sanders. (LC)

LITHOGRAPH OF THE DITCH AT FORT SANDERS, LOOKING NORTH. Orlando Poe liked this image so much that he included it in his article in *Battles and Leaders.* This skilled lithographer was able to translate visual information into a printable format for 1890s technology. None of the detail is lost; in fact, some details are clarified in this second generation of the visual information. (AC)

A WINTER DAY IN EAST TENNESSEE. This beautiful image by George Barnard shows the severity of the winter of 1864. Taken in Chattanooga, it documents the extreme conditions encountered by Longstreet's often-barefoot troops. Clothed for a Virginia summer, they found themselves enduring the winter shown in this picture; overcoats, blankets, tents, and boots were in short supply. Federal troops were little better off. Numerous accounts mention the bloodstained snow left in the wake of the marching Confederate troops. (LC)

GEN. AMBROSE BURNSIDE. This portrait of the Union commander was taken at the Schleier studio in Knoxville and was in the carte de visite collection of Scotia Temple. Burnside was very well liked and respected by his soldiers and the civilian population in Knoxville. He in turn felt a great responsibility toward the people, determined to secure the territory he had entered. His performance at Campbell's Station and the defense of Knoxville were exemplary. (SPCL)

GEN. JAMES LONGSTREET. Lee's "Old War Horse" did not make a good showing in his first venture into independent command. Infighting among his officers, blame, acrimony, and finally courts-martials for several of his once-trusted subordinates came out of the Knoxville Campaign. The loss of hundreds of his finest troops at the Battle of Fort Sanders won no advantage and is generally viewed as a blunder. (LC)

LT. SAMUEL N. BENJAMIN. At West Point with Poe and Gen. William P. Sanders, Benjamin was only a lieutenant when he commanded the artillery position inside Fort Sanders. An artillerist of great ability, he is credited with taking out the sharpshooters in the tower in Longstreet's headquarters at Bleak House with one shot. He also devised the shells with shortened fuses, personally lighting and throwing them over the parapet into the massed Confederates in the ditch below. (SPCL)

GEN. EDWARD FERRERO. Lieutenant Benjamin wrote in his official report that Ferrero never came out of the telegraph bombproof during the Battle of Fort Sanders. While discrediting a superior officer is never seen as good form, the documented similar behavior of Ferrero at Petersburg may substantiate Benjamin's account of his performance here; nevertheless, Ferrero returned to his civilian job of dance master after the war without serious repercussions. (MM)

Gen. Lafayette McLaws. One of the defenders on the heights at the Battle of Fredericksburg, McLaws and Longstreet had long fought together. McLaws was chosen to lead the assault at Fort Sanders, selecting the brigades of Wofford, Humphrey, and Bryan. He was subsequently unjustly blamed for the disastrous attack. McLaws requested a court-martial to clear his name, but despite being exonerated, he was reassigned to Savannah and face Sherman in his future "March to the Sea." (LC)

Col. E. Porter Alexander. At West Point with William P. Sanders and Orlando Poe, Alexander had made a name for himself in the Signal Corps and as an artillerist. He reported on Confederate engineer Danville Leadbetter's inability to read the ground and was disappointed in the diminished role of artillery in the attack on Fort Sanders. After the battle, he and Poe shared a flask, and he discovered that he had been firing on his friend Sanders in the action of November 18, 1863. (AC)

Gen. Bushrod Johnson. Raised as a Quaker in Ohio, Johnson graduated from West Point, a classmate of Union generals George Thomas and William T. Sherman. Teaching at Western Military Institute in Nashville when the war broke out, he was one of the few generals reared in the North who fought for the Confederacy. His early record was highly commended, especially at Chickamauga, but his performance at Petersburg and Sailor's Creek left Gen. Robert E. Lee unimpressed. (SPCL)

Gen. Orville E. Babcock. A West Point engineer, Babcock played a major role in the defenses of Knoxville. After the battle, he was one of two officers who walked down Kingston Road with a flag of truce being offered by General Burnside. The rest of the day was spent exchanging the dead, wounded, and prisoners. At 7:00 p.m., when the truce ended, both armies returned to their lines and resumed the siege. (LC)

Col. G. Moxley Sorrel. As Longstreet's adjutant, it was Sorrell who went to meet the Union officers bearing the flag of truce to negotiate the terms for his superiors. He later recalled the East Tennessee Campaign with candor and in great detail in a memoir called *Fighting for the Confederacy*. (SPCL)

Cpl. John Watkins. One of the few enlisted men whose Knoxville experiences are well documented, Watkins was an artillerist in the 19th Ohio Infantry. He witnessed the battle firsthand and described the horrors of the slaughter in the ditch. He returned for the Blue and Gray Reunion in 1895 and commented on how much the fortifications had deteriorated. (MM)

Two

FORTIFICATION

In November 1863, as the Confederate army of Gen. James Longstreet advanced north from Chattanooga toward Knoxville, Union engineer Captain Orlando Poe was ordered to fortify the town. Knowing that the heights on the south side of the river were vital to any successful defense, his first task was the installation of a pontoon bridge. Next, he organized both Union and Confederate residents of the town, including several hundred African Americans, to assist in digging the essential fortifications. Pursued by the Rebels, General Burnside's exhausted troops made it from Lenoir City to the developing fortress. After two hours of sleep, they were handed shovels and told to dig for their lives as Poe directed arriving regiments and artillery into position.

For nearly two weeks within the safety of the skillfully defended town, the Federals continued to prepare for the imminent attack by advancing Rebel forces. The defenders created several miles of forts, batteries, and rifle trenches. The encircling and also entrenching opposition planned to starve them out, but because of unfolding military events to the south, the Rebels were ordered to pick the weakest point and break into the fortress. When it came to predicting where the inevitable attack would take place, both Federal engineers and the Confederate generals were aware of the vulnerable location of Fort Sanders, and Chief Engineer Orlando Poe did his brilliant best to compensate. The failure of the best troops of the CSA to take the town proved the success of his efforts.

In March 1864, Captain Poe returned to Knoxville with Army contract photographer George Barnard. Using emerging photographic technology, they captured on glass plates the details of the town and its defenses to include with Poe's official written report. A new era of panoramic documentary photography had begun. Visiting Gen. William T. Sherman recognized the talents of both Poe and Barnard. As a result of their achievements in Knoxville, both men were handpicked by Sherman for the tactical challenges of the Atlanta Campaign and subsequent March to the Sea.

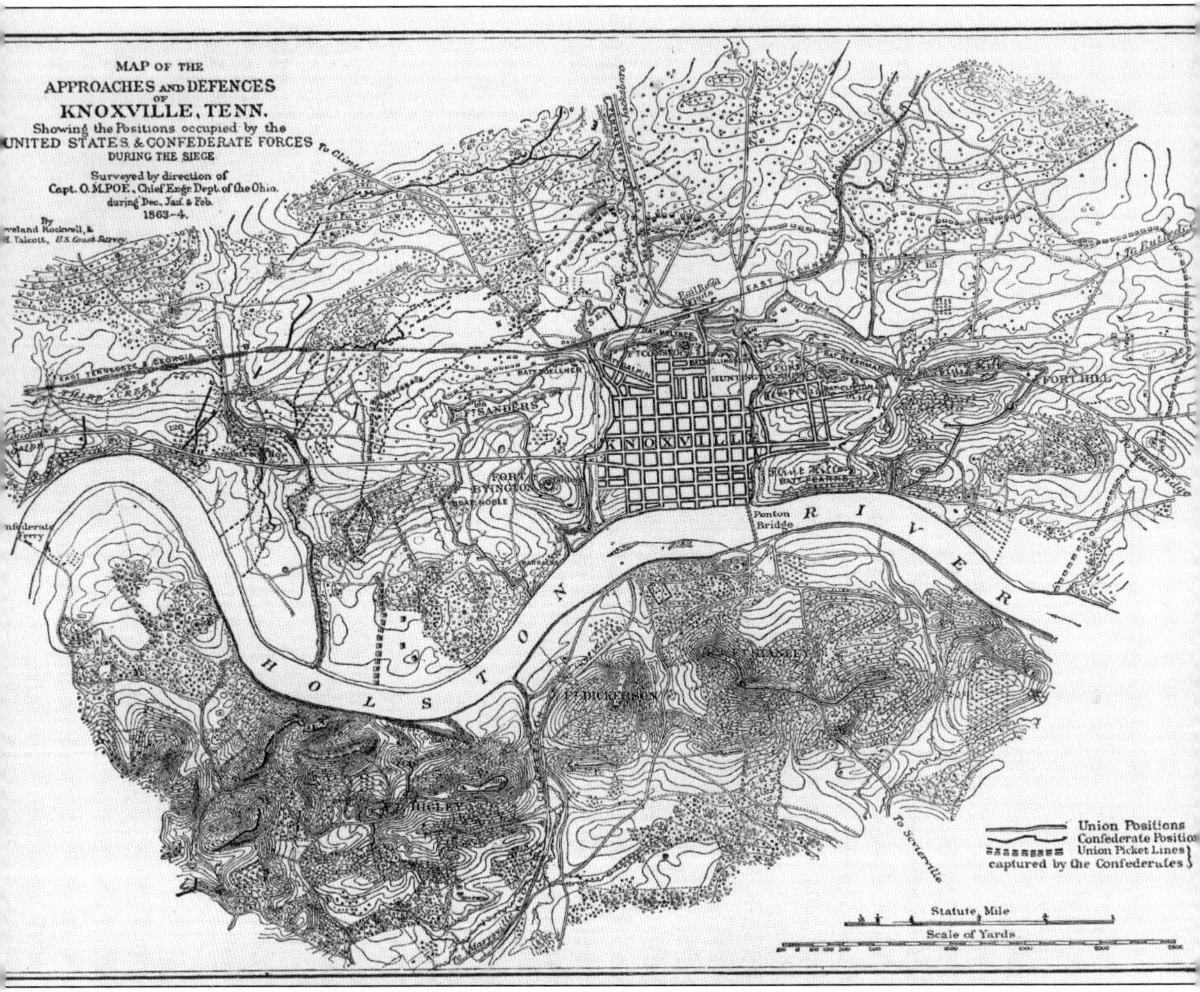

"Map of the Approaches and Defences of Knoxville." Upon receiving the printed version in March 1864, Orlando Poe stated simply, "It is a beautiful map." As accurate today as it was then, this topographical map shows the natural terrain of Knoxville and the fortifications built by both the Union and the Confederates during the siege of Knoxville. The locations of the railroad, Kingston Pike (the main east-west road), the river, and the downtown street grid have barely changed in 150 years. (LC)

Poe and Babcock at Fort Sanders. It is interesting to compare this stereo card to the image on the cover of this book. Note that they have swapped positions. Both men contributed to the defensive works created so well and so quickly. Their careers as young and talented West Point engineers would be launched from their achievements in East Tennessee. (LC)

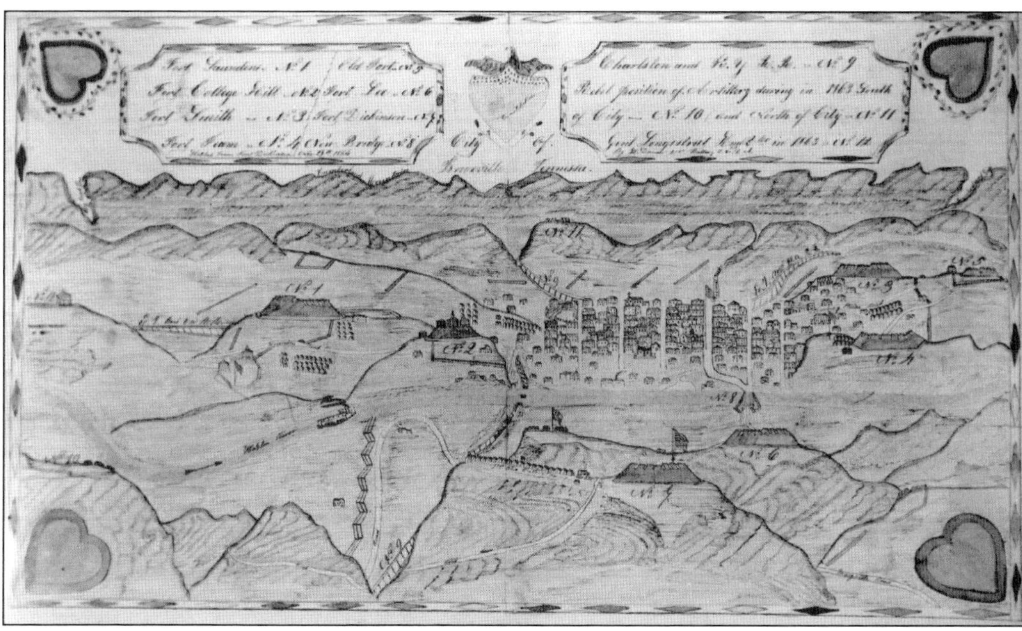

A Private's Sketch of Fortified Knoxville. In November 1864, Pvt. Henry Doman of the 21st Battery of the Ohio Light Artillery created this detailed sketch of the town from his encampment on the heights at Fort Dickerson. Many delightful details, such a train and a riverboat, are included, along with very accurate renderings of the streets, buildings, and fortified positions. (AC)

Gen. Orlando Poe. A West Point–trained engineer, Poe enjoyed the complete confidence of his commanding officer, General Burnside. Although he had attained the rank of general of volunteers in a Michigan regiment, as seen in this portrait, Congress did not approve his commission. When he arrived in Knoxville in the fall of 1863, his rank was captain. By 1865, he would once again climb to the rank of general. (LC)

Pontoon Bridge. The only image of Poe's pontoon bridge is in the background of this lithograph of the Holston River. The need to connect the town with the defensible heights on the south side of the river was critical. General Sanders and his mounted infantry used this bridge to defend the town against a CSA attack from the south on November 15, 1863. The knobs were fortified, and the artillery was positioned as a result of this temporary conveyance. (AC)

Looking West from Mabry's Hill. Photographer George Barnard captured the town looking west from Mabry's Hill on the far east of the Union line. To protect the northern approach, Poe dammed First and Second Creeks. The water barrier in the vicinity of what is now the Old City can be seen in the far right background. On the left edge is a graded road. At higher magnification a pipe can been seen in the soldier's mouth. (LC)

Panorama from the University Cupola. Poe and Barnard climbed to the cupola of East Tennessee University to take the next seven frames; they form a complete 360-degree view. This first image looks northwest and shows Fort Sanders in the center. The pond is a sinkhole near today's University of Tennessee College of Law. Kingston Pike goes across the frame crossed by a rifle trench. The house on the left no longer exists. (LC)

NORTH FROM THE UNIVERSITY. The home in the middle on Kingston Road belonged to lawyer Hugh Lawson White who ran for president in the 1830s. Note the tents along the northern defensive line. Sharp's Gap, where the railroad then and now and present-day Interstate 75 pass through the ridge on their way north is visible. Parallel tent rows can be seen on the grounds of the Deaf and Dumb Asylum on the far right. (LC)

NORTHEAST FROM THE UNIVERSITY. The occupied city of Knoxville can be seen over the roof of the university where photographer Barnard stood in March 1864. The spire of Second Presbyterian Church, where General Sanders was buried, is visible in the center. A fuzzy courthouse tower can be seen on the far right. (LC)

SOUTHEAST FROM THE UNIVERSITY. The recently completed military bridge to the west of the mouth of First Creek spans the Holston (present-day Tennessee) River. Note the cannon and caissons in the yard of the university president's "White House," roughly where Neyland Stadium stands today. The island in the river illustrates the difficulty for river traffic. (LC)

SOUTH FROM THE UNIVERSITY. On the prominent knobs, Forts Stanley and Dickerson are clearly seen. Chapman Highway (US 441) passes between these two heights today. Note the almost treeless slopes of the knobs; shelter, cooking, and defensive line of sight dictated the clearing. The piers, which stand in the river to this day, support the railroad bridge under construction in 1864. (LC)

Southwest from the University. Fort Higley, farthest west of the Union fortification on the south side of the river, is visible in this view. Note the neat rows of tents near where the McClung Museum on Circle Park Drive sits today. The small white building with five doors has not been identified in any of the old prints, but one good guess is that it was the privy for the university buildings just up the hill. (LC)

West from the University. Well-traveled roads cross the treeless expanse. The large homes in the distance were inevitably caught up in the fighting. Melrose, on the right, was "loop-holed" by the defenders according to Union maps. Holes were punched through the newly constructed walls for sharpshooters. Battery Noble was located on this site. (LC)

Melrose, Home of Columbus Powell. Now long gone, this stately home called Melrose sat on the hilltop where a dormitory still bears its name. Owned successively by the Powell, Temple, and O'Connor families, the Melrose estate had a pond and long, curving drive. Joseph Mabry III famously murdered owner Thomas O'Connor on Gay Street in the 1880s. (MM)

University Buildings on the Hill. These buildings were actually incorporated in the fortifications called Fort Byington. The artillery position was manned by Maj. Jacob Roemer's New York Battery and was heavily shelled before the attack on Fort Sanders. All the university buildings were used as hospitals by both sides and had to be completely renovated after the war before classes could resume. (MM)

FROM SOUTH OF THE RIVER, LOOKING WEST. Poe and Barnard used Fort Stanley as the location from which to take a four-frame scan of the north side of the river. Looking west, the naturally hilly terrain is evident. With magnification, the tents of the Union encampment are visible on Fort Dickerson. The meandering river is on the far right; a Confederate ferry was just out of sight. (LC)

FROM FORT STANLEY, LOOKING NORTHWEST. The army barracks at Circle Park are clear in this image, as are the university buildings on the hill. Fort Sanders is just behind the university on the far right. Military equipment and tents can be seen in several locations. The excavation in the foreground is for the installation of a railroad bed. The piers for the new railroad bridge can be seen on the far right. (LC)

FROM FORT STANLEY, LOOKING NORTH ACROSS THE RIVER. Almost all of downtown Knoxville can be seen here. The completed military bridge is visible on the far right. Sharp's Gap is prominent on the horizon. The white tower of the courthouse sits between Gay Street and then Prince Street. The pillars of First Presbyterian Church are just above the bridge on the right. (LC)

FROM FORT STANLEY, LOOKING NORTHEAST. The encampment along the north face of the hill on which Fort Stanley sits is located in the safest position. With their backs to the well-defended city, troops are protected from fire resulting from an attack from the south. Note the hog facility on the riverbank. On the far right are the easternmost lines of the Union defenses. (LC)

ENCAMPMENT ON SLOPE OF FORT STANLEY. Some unintentionally documented details of camp life can be appreciated in this image. The documentation of the construction of shelters with log walls, a canvas roof, and brick and metal chimneys can aid archaeologists interpret their findings from camp excavations. Note the pot and lid inside the box in the left foreground. It also appears as if a blanket has been hung out to dry. (LC)

LITHOGRAPHIC PANORAMA FROM *HARPER'S WEEKLY*. In this rendering, the town is simplified and the fortifications exaggerated. Fort Sanders is to the left of the university buildings. Extensive earthmoving went into the creations of Fort Huntington-Smith and Fort Hill on the east side of Knoxville. The Army continued to work on the fortifications throughout the war, turning Knoxville into "the keep of East Tennessee." (AC)

Lithograph of Fort Stanley. The details here show the construction of the fort, the clearing of all the trees on the summit, and an encampment on the saddle of the ridge (upper left). This image was included in the *Battles and Leaders* article on Knoxville by Orlando Poe. (AC)

Vital Railroad Bridge. This bridge over the Holston River in Strawberry Plains east of Knoxville was burned and rebuilt four times during the war. It was the bridge burned by Colonel Sanders during his June 1863 raid. Note the fine hilltop fort just to the left of the stone pillar. To the right of the pillar, one can see a tripod camera and one of the few known field images of George Barnard. (LC)

Orlando Metcalfe Poe. Accomplished as an engineer, designer, builder, and documentarian, Poe was convinced that his work in Knoxville would make his career; however, the course of the war drew attention away from these accomplishments. Gen. William T. Sherman handpicked Poe and photographer George Barnard to accompany him on his developing plan to go south to Atlanta and then on to the sea, and a whole new phase of his career began. (Courtesy of Dennis Urban.)

SURRENDER AT APPOMATTOX, APRIL 1865. While no photographs were taken of the proceedings at the McLean House, multiple first-person accounts place Orville Babcock on Robert E. Lee's right. As a valued member of Gen. Ulysses S. Grant's staff, Babcock met Lee outside of town and accompanied him to the location selected for the signing of the surrender. In this image, Babcock is fourth from the left. (LC)

GEN. WILLIAM T. SHERMAN. When an exhausted Sherman arrived in Knoxville on December 4, 1863, he was none too happy to find Burnside and his staff enjoying a feast at the home of lawyer Oliver P. Temple. Despite the fact that the ladies had searched high and low to gather enough food together to honor Sherman's arrival, the general never had any affection for East Tennessee and could not wait to return to Chattanooga. (SPCL)

General Sherman and Staff in Atlanta. In this Barnard photograph, Orlando Poe sits behind the cannon barrel in civilian clothes, while Sherman leans on the cannon. Poe and his Michigan engineers would be vital to the successful destruction of railroads and other military targets. The engineers under his command perfected the efficient building of corduroy roads and pontoon bridges on the March to the Sea. (LC)

Three

GETTING TO KNOXVILLE

Over two years into a still unfolding Civil War, troops on both sides had become veterans of numerous battles. From general to private, many of the soldiers meeting in Knoxville had fought each other before. Most notably, Union general Ambrose Burnside and Confederate general James Longstreet had met at Fredericksburg, Virginia. In November 1862, Longstreet held the high ground at Marye's Heights, while Burnside ordered thousands of troops into deadly fire. Even engineer Orlando Poe had led a Michigan brigade at Fredericksburg. After that disaster, which was clearly Burnside's responsibility, he was replaced and sent west to finally enact Lincoln's plan to liberate East Tennessee.

Longstreet, after the July 1863 Confederate defeat at Gettysburg, was sent south with John Bell Hood's and Lafayette McLaws's divisions to reinforce Gen. Braxton Bragg, arriving just in time to influence the Confederate victory at Chickamauga. As newly appointed commanding general of the defeated Union troops, Ulysses S. Grant sat besieged in Chattanooga when Bragg inexplicably ordered Longstreet north to retake Knoxville. When Burnside learned of the advance of Longstreet's army, he conferred by telegram with Grant. They decided that Burnside would continue to lure Longstreet away from Chattanooga while Grant defeated a weakened Bragg, and then Grant would come to Burnside's aid.

Unfortunately for Longstreet, he had ordered Gen. Joseph Wheeler's cavalry ahead to take Knoxville from the south side of the river. Gen. William P. Sanders challenged Wheeler's advance before finally falling back to the cover of Union artillery. Wheeler returned to Longstreet too late to influence the results of the action at Campbell's Station, where the two armies had first clashed. Winning a finely executed artillery duel, Union troops dashed to the relative safety of the town being hastily fortified by Captain Poe.

Cavalry officer Gen. William P. Sanders, a friend and West Point classmate of Poe, was asked by Burnside to delay the pursuing CSA west of town while the fortifications were constructed. After a valiant 24-hour stand, he was mortally wounded. The Union line fell back into the greatly strengthened town, and the siege began.

Burnside and Longstreet Had Met Before. It was from this superior position called Marye's Heights that Longstreet's defenders mowed down wave after wave of infantry ordered forward by Burnside at the Battle of Fredericksburg in December 1862. Almost a year later in Knoxville, their positions would be reversed as Burnside defended from the heights of Fort Sanders and Longstreet's fine assault troops marched against an impregnable position. (LC)

Gen. James Brevard Kershaw. Kershaw's South Carolina troops were behind the wall at Marye's Heights in Fredericksburg. In Knoxville, he made his headquarters at the Armstrong home at Crescent Bend on Kingston Road. His men defended the artillery position across Kingston Pike, recently excavated by the University of Tennessee's Archaeological Research Laboratory. It was near this location that General Sanders was mortally wounded holding back advancing CSA troops. (SPCL)

GEN. ORLANDO POE. At the Battle of Fredericksburg, Gen. Orlando Poe led a Michigan brigade under General Burnside; luckily for him, it was not one of those sent into Longstreet's firepower. Poe was soon transferred to Ohio and the 9th Army Corps. When Burnside marched south to East Tennessee, Poe, well supplied with picks and shovels, accompanied him as chief engineer. (Courtesy of Dennis Urban.)

GEN. JAMES LONGSTREET. Perhaps looking for independent command to replace General Bragg as commanding general in Chattanooga, in September 1863 Longstreet came west with his troops on one of the most unusual train journeys of any war. Because Knoxville was held by the Union, small railroads throughout North Carolina, South Carolina, and Georgia had to be used to transport his army. They nevertheless arrived at the Battle of Chickamauga in time to influence the Confederate victory. (SPCL)

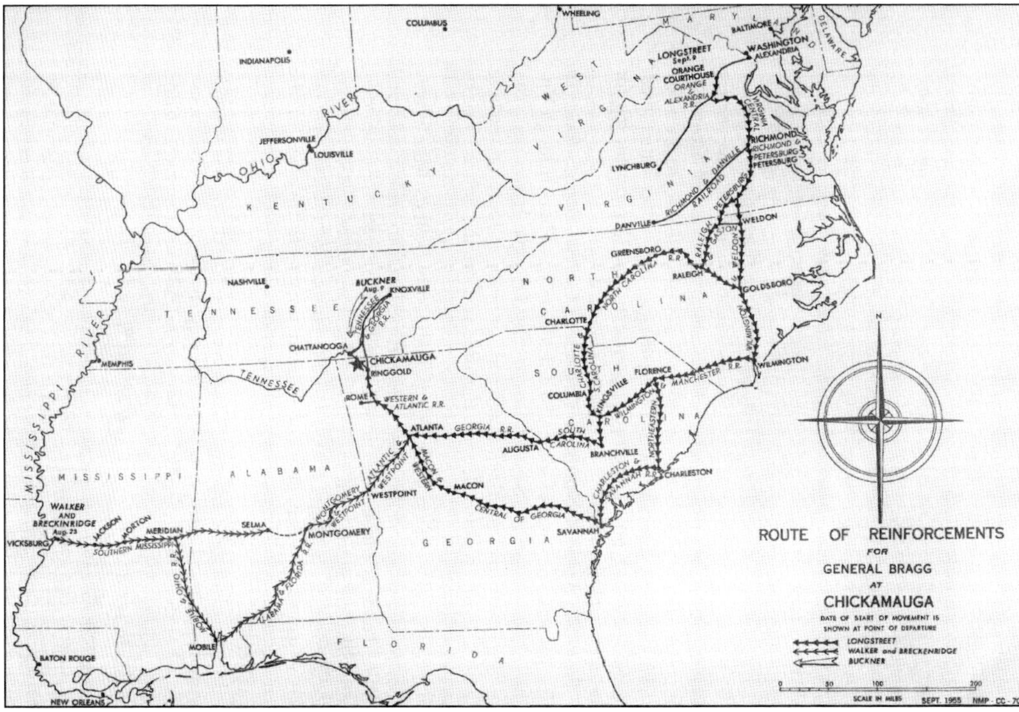

Map of Longstreet's Journey South. The details of the route taken by Longstreet with Hood's and McLaws's divisions as well as other reinforcements for General Bragg are presented in this 1950s map. On the journey, often troops arrived on one train, disembarked, marched across town, and departed on another rail line of a different size gauge. (AC)

Gen. Braxton Bragg. Few generals in the CSA earned as little respect as Braxton Bragg. After a definitive victory at Chickamauga to which Longstreet contributed, Bragg surrounded Federal troops who had retreated to Chattanooga. Bragg, with dubious military justification, then decided to rid himself of a critical Longstreet by ordering him north to retake Knoxville. (LC)

Longstreet's Sharpshooters. In this *Harper's Weekly* illustration, the rugged terrain of East Tennessee is highlighted as well as the famous sharpshooters who traveled with Longstreet's army. Some of those favored with the fine British Whitworth rifle saw action in Knoxville. Distinctive hexagonal Whitworth bullets have been found at Confederate positions around town. (AC)

Gen. Ambrose Burnside. In Burnside's defense, before the Union disaster at Fredericksburg, he had turned down Lincoln's request that he replace Gen. George McClellan as commanding general. Burnside did not think he was ready for the position and then proved it. Lincoln, however, knew that Burnside was a valuable leader, so sent him to Ohio to the impending invasion of East Tennessee. (SPCL)

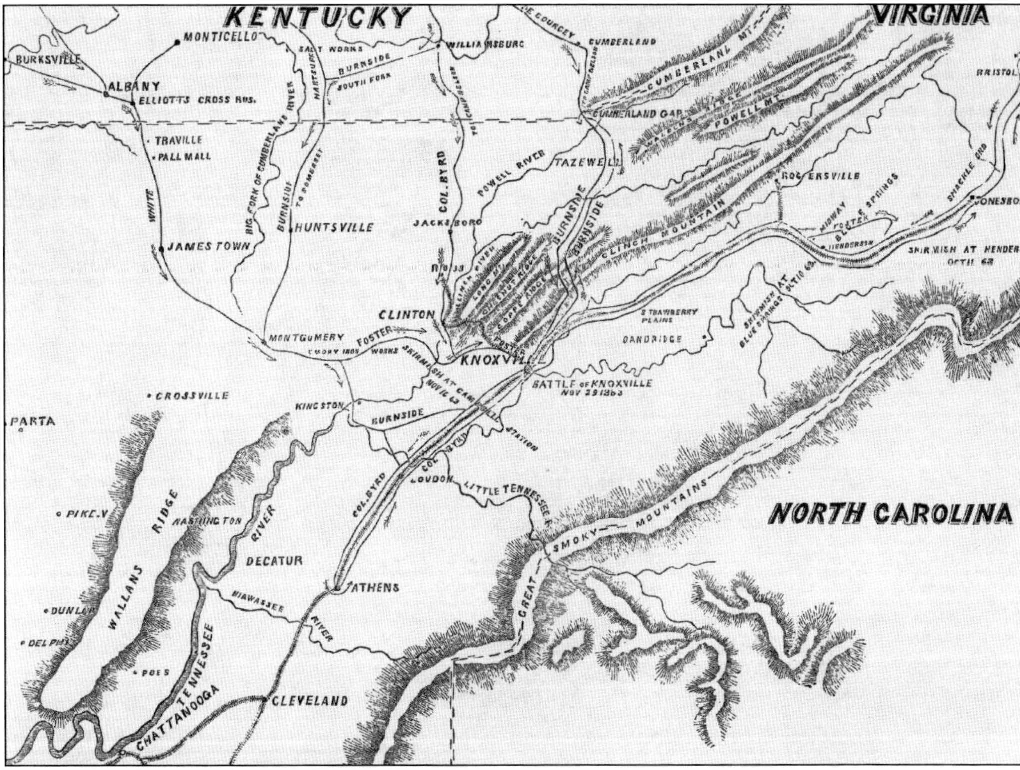

Map of Burnside's Route to Knoxville. This detailed map appeared in *Harper's Weekly* in 1866. After being contested by both sides since the beginning of the war, the Cumberland Gap was bypassed altogether by Burnside's invading army. In September, Burnside won possession of it from the south when Confederate general John Fraser surrendered to superior numbers. (AC)

Gen. William Rosecrans. A leader with outstanding abilities and glaring shortcomings, Rosecrans's miscalculations led to his disastrous defeat at Chickamauga. He was forced to retreat to Chattanooga, where he sat under siege, virtually incapacitated. Gen. George "the Rock of Chickamauga" Thomas replaced him until the arrival of Gen. Ulysses S. Grant. (SPCL)

Gen. Ulysses S. Grant. The victor at Fort Donelson, Shiloh, and Vicksburg, Grant made his reputation in the Western Theater. He was ordered by Lincoln to replace Rosecrans at Chattanooga and save the situation—this he did with extraordinary success. He and Burnside immediately trusted each other's abilities and together planned to keep Bragg's dispersed troops from reassembling. (LC)

Routes Taken North to Knoxville. Burnside could have engaged Longstreet's troops as they crossed the Tennessee River at Hough's Ferry; instead, he decided to act as bait, leading them farther away from Chattanooga. Burnside personally led his dispersed troops from Lenoir back to Knoxville in the pouring rain over impassible roads. The nonparallel paths of the two armies crossed at Campbell's Station, where a battle took place on November 16, 1863. (Courtesy of Steve Dean.)

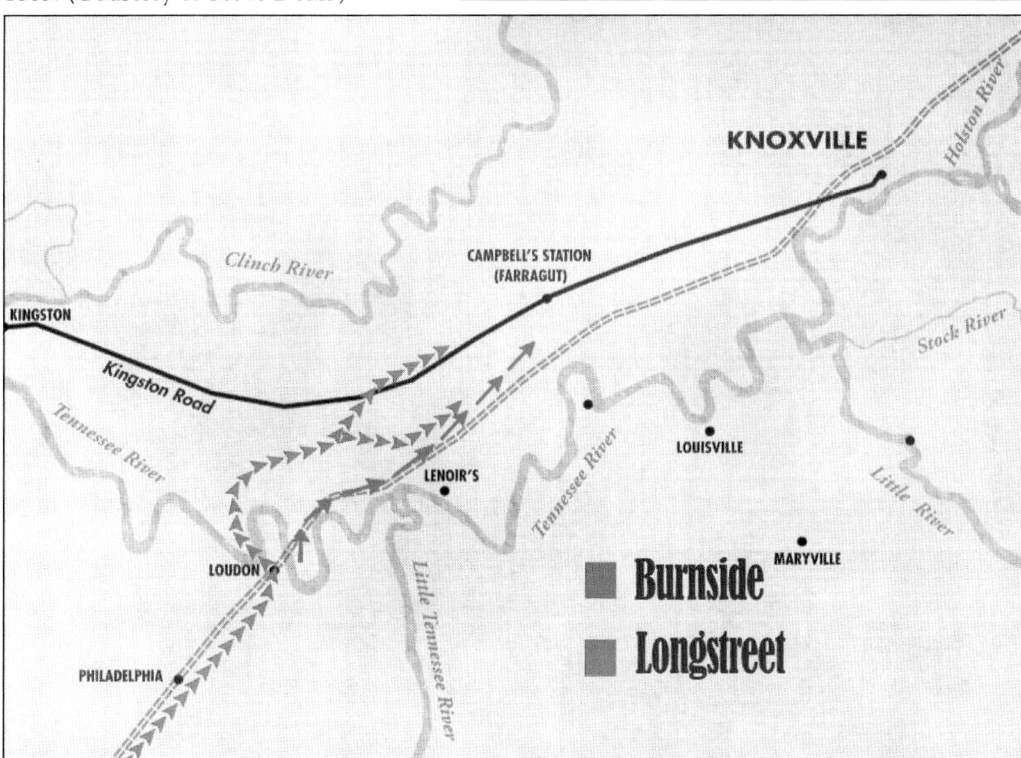

THE BATTLE OF CAMPBELL'S STATION, A PAINTING BY PAUL LONG. This well-researched depiction of the battle in what is present-day Farragut shows the final stages of the artillery duel. The Union continues to hold the road against the Confederate attack; the Federal supply train, without artillery and ammunition wagons, is on its way to Knoxville by this time. The two houses shown along the main road (Kingston Road) still stand today. (Courtesy of Paul Long.)

FRONT PAGE OF THE *NEW YORK TRIBUNE*. News of the action in East Tennessee was reported in Northern papers despite the difficulty in getting the stories out of the mountainous area. A December 7, 1863, story shows this accurate map and reports the action at Campbell's Station. The two houses still standing today are indicated along the main road to Knoxville. (AC)

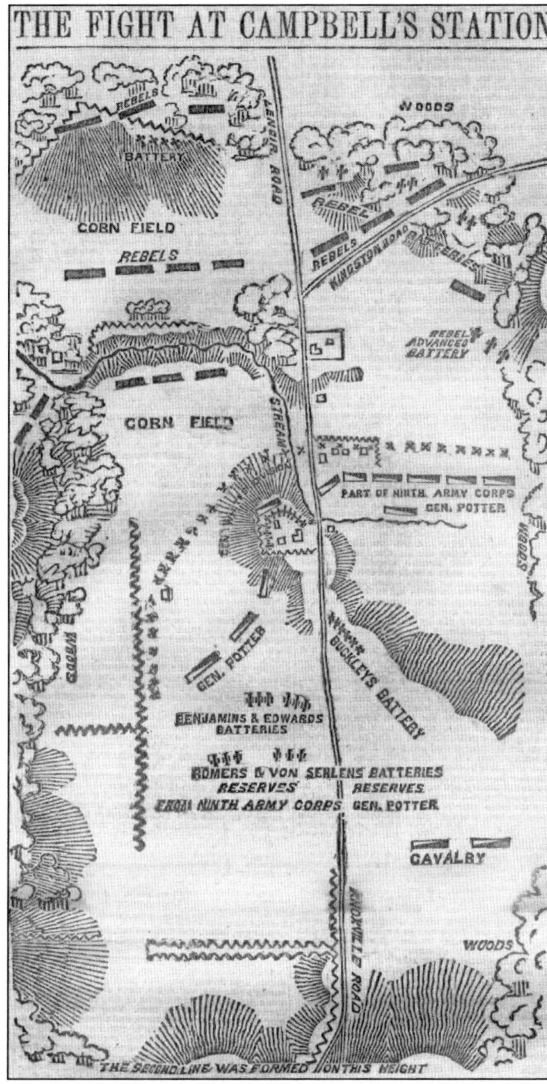

GEN. MICAH JENKINS. Gen. John B. Hood made the trip from Virginia to Georgia but was wounded at the Battle of Chickamauga and did not go on to Knoxville. The leadership of his command was fought over by Gen. Micah Jenkins and Gen. Evander Law, contributing to Longstreet's many Knoxville campaign troubles. (SPCL)

Gen. Evander Law. This young general had seniority over Jenkins and thought the leadership of Hood's division should go to himself. Longstreet, who favored Micah Jenkins, felt that Law intentionally misled his troops at Campbell's Station so that Jenkins would not get credit for a successful attack. Law was later court-martialed at Longstreet's request but exonerated of the charges. (SPCL)

Gen. William P. Sanders. The gallant, recently promoted General Sanders was detached by Burnside to protect the southern approach to Knoxville. Longstreet sent his cavalry to take the city from this attack point, but the defense offered by Sanders, his mounted infantry, and the newly positioned artillery south of the river prevented the CSA from taking the town on November 15 through the "back door." (Courtesy of Dennis Urban.)

MORGAN'S RAIDERS. Burnside and his army in Ohio were prevented from getting to East Tennessee sooner by several major obstacles. One was the invasion of Ohio by Morgan's Raiders. Colonel Sanders was instrumental in the capture and imprisonment of Morgan, a relation of the wealthy McClung family in Knoxville. (AC)

GEN. JOHN HUNT MORGAN. This renowned raider was related to the McClung family in Knoxville. When he escaped from an Ohio prison in 1863, he returned to the friendlier territory of East Tennessee. Having angered Gen. Braxton Bragg by exceeding his orders by going too far north, he found himself somewhat restricted in his new location. He was killed in Greeneville in 1864 by Union cavalry that included the command of Col. John B. Brownlow, William's younger son. (LC)

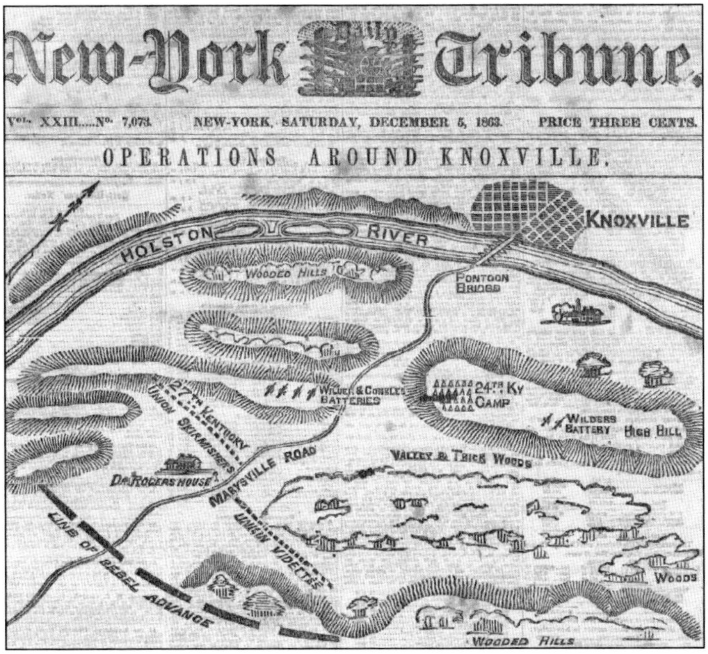

ACTION SOUTH OF THE RIVER. The *New York Tribune* ran coverage of the action south of the river in Knoxville as front-page news on December 5, 1863. An accurate map of the territory fought over by the cavalries of Wheeler and Sanders is a great source of information as to where specific commands were posted prior to the siege of Knoxville. (AC)

"FIGHTING JOE" WHEELER. Although he was raised primarily in the North, Wheeler's sympathies were all Southern. Calling himself "the War Child" according to one newspaper account, Gen. Joseph Wheeler was small, young, and courageous but lacked good judgment in some circumstances. During the siege, his cavalry was posted in East Knoxville. (LC)

Gen. Joseph Wheeler. After the Civil War, Wheeler once again entered the Army as a US volunteer in the Spanish-American War and then the Philippine-American War. This stereo image shows an aging, white-bearded Wheeler with Teddy Roosevelt at, perhaps, San Juan Hill. Unlike most Confederate generals, Wheeler is buried in Arlington National Cemetery in Washington, DC. (AC)

Reverse of Sanders's Carte de Visite. Orlando Poe and "Doc" Sanders were friends at West Point and real comrades in arms during the campaign in East Tennessee. In Rheatown, they tried to convince Burnside they knew a better way for cavalry to attack, but Burnside called them "hotheads." Sanders's death on November 19 deeply affected his friend. At Poe's suggestion, the most prominent fort in Knoxville was named in Sanders's honor. (Courtesy of Dennis Urban.)

Lamar House. After being mortally wounded while holding back the CSA troops west of town on November 18, 1863, Sanders was taken to the Lamar House, Knoxville's best hotel. Burnside sat by his bedside as he lay dying. His funeral was held in the middle of the night; supposedly, the troops were not told of his death, but several letters and diaries indicate that the sad news was widely known. (MM)

Four

Confederate Occupation

Even before Tennessee had declared its independence from the United States, Confederate soldiers were camped just outside of Knoxville. When the vote was taken, the town split almost evenly for and against union except for the votes cast by the occupying troops. In Knox County and the surrounding counties, Union loyalty was predominant. Under the command of the first Confederate general, former Knoxvillian Felix Zollicoffer, a tolerant attitude was shown toward Unionists. However, with the ill-advised and unsupported railroad bridge–burning incident of November 1861, both military and civilian authorities came down harshly on Union sympathizers. Drumhead court-martials, hanging, imprisonment, conscription, property confiscation, and general oppression became common.

Outspoken editor William Brownlow, originally allowed to publish his pro-Union newspaper, found himself imprisoned and then he and his family exiled. He began a sojourn in the North decrying the treatment of loyal citizens in East Tennessee, and he soon published a best-selling book with numerous illustrations. And he did not hesitate to name names.

In 1862, Knoxville became the center of justice for members of the James J. Andrews's locomotive raid who were imprisoned in town. The story of their escapade behind Confederate lines reads like fiction. Coming to Knoxville on the train, they were escorted by some of John Hunt Morgan's men who were equally concerned about the legal issues posed by undercover operatives. Seven of the raiders were tried in the Knoxville Courthouse with Unionist lawyers O.P. Temple and John Baxter representing the defendants.

The constant presence of Confederate troops did make the city safer than the countryside, but the civilian population constantly feared invasion by Union troops massing on the Kentucky border only 60 miles away. In December 1862, Gen. Samuel Carter staged a raid on railroad bridges in upper East Tennessee. In June 1863, Col. William P. Sanders and 1,500 cavalry harassed civilians in Lenoir City and conducted an artillery bombardment of Knoxville. At this encounter, many civilians manned artillery positions, and Confederate Pleasant McClung, grandson of two of the founders of the town, was killed by cannon fire.

GEN. FELIX ZOLLICOFFER. This popular Tennessean, and one-time Knoxvillian, took a conciliatory position toward Unionists in Knoxville, thinking most of them would come around, as he had, to support the Confederacy. When he was killed at the Battle of Mill Springs, Kentucky, in January 1862, he had already been replaced with a hard-liner Gen. George Crittenden. The Richmond government felt that harsher control was necessary. (LC)

The Battle of Mill Springs, Kentucky, January 29, 1862. This Currier and Ives print shows the disorganized retreat of the generally poorly armed and trained Confederate troops. While the casualties of this Union victory were small compared with all that were to come, the death of the popular Zollicoffer and the retreat of CSA troops were of real concern to Knoxville's Confederates. (LC)

The Bridge Burning of November 1861. Railroad bridges were the targets of armed groups of Unionists who were convinced that their action would be followed by a speedy invasion by Federal troops from Kentucky. The plan had been approved and funded by Lincoln working with East Tennessean reverend William Carter. At the last minute, invading troops led by Gens. George Thomas and William Sherman were ordered to halt, and the unfortunate bridge burners were left to Confederate justice. This is a Barnard photograph of Flat Creek, east of Knoxville. (LC)

Life or Death Decisions. Particularly after the institution of the Confederate draft, all men in East Tennessee had to decide whether to fight for one side or the other—there was no neutrality. Many men made the dangerous trip to Kentucky to enlist in the Union army. Some tried to hide out in the mountains, but most eventually ended up in some army or in jail. (AC)

GEN. DANVILLE LEADBETTER, CSA. Early in the war, Leadbetter served in Greeneville and Knoxville. From Maine and trained as a West Point engineer, he would nevertheless dispense some of the most severe reprisals against the Unionists involved in the bridge-burning incident. (SPCL)

***SKETCHES OF THE RISE, PROGRESS, AND DECLINE OF SECESSION* BY WILLIAM G. BROWNLOW.** When Brownlow and his family were exiled to the North, he became an author and lecturer with a powerful story to tell. His dramatically illustrated book, including details of the fate of bridge burners and his time in jail, became a best seller. Here, men found guilty of bridge burning were hanged, and their bodies were publicly displayed. (AC)

A Young Unionist at the Gallows. Sitting atop his own coffin, this young husband and father convicted of bridge burning is depicted saying goodbye to his wife and children. Arrest, imprisonment, and hanging were the consequences of this ill-advised and unsupported violence against Confederate authority. (AC)

The Gallows. Located somewhere near the later Louisville and Nashville Railroad Depot on present-day Henley Street, then the outskirts of town, the gallows became a symbol of oppression for the Unionists. Here, two men, probably Jacob Harmon and his son, are hanged by the military to the cheers of the crowd. Brownlow was in the same jail as these prisoners. (AC)

The Fighting Parson William G. Brownlow. Already an outspoken and controversial newspaper editor, Brownlow was in 1861 allowed to continue publishing despite his avowed Union support. He was in hiding in the mountains when the bridge burning occurred, probably without his prior knowledge. Granted permission to go north by Richmond authorities, he was nevertheless arrested and imprisoned by Knoxville civilian Confederate authorities, some of his prewar enemies. (AC)

Parson Brownlow in Jail. Here, the parson is seen being greeted by imprisoned Unionists in the Knoxville jail. Many of these men, according to Brownlow, were arrested simply for holding Union sentiments and not for any overt acts against the Confederate government. They endured cold, over-crowded, and disease-ridden conditions and were short on rations. (AC)

UNIONISTS GOING TO PRISON. Many of the men arrested in the fall of 1861 were sent to prison in Tuscaloosa, Alabama, with the old or sickly never seeing home again. This is a fairly good illustration of the unusual architecture of the long-gone "Castle Fox" Jail, located on Hill and Main Streets downtown. It was named for jailor Robert Fox, a Confederate. Later, under Union control, he was jailed in the institution bearing his name. (AC)

VIOLENCE AGAINST THE CITIZENS. Brownlow had personally witnessed some of the events illustrated in his book, and his jail mates reported others to him. The depiction of the harassment of Unionist civilians by pro-Confederate gangs was probably accurate. (AC)

Brownlow's Revenge, Robert Reynolds. Brownlow had no problem singling out men who had caused his personal trials. In this case, Knoxvillian Robert Reynolds, appointed as a commissioner for the Confederate states, is shown as a public drunkard and object of amusement. (AC)

Another Prewar Enemy, Attorney Crozier Ramsey. Brownlow seems to take pleasure in publicizing an event involving Crozier Ramsey and a Confederate encampment. In this image, this son of Dr. J.G.M. Ramsey is marched out of camp with his hands tied behind his back wearing a sign around his neck stating, "Thief." The Confederate probably reported details of the incident quite differently. (AC)

James Andrews, Union Spy and Railroad Raider. The adventures of Union operatives James Andrews and his raiders have been widely reported and misreported. Like the bridge burners, their mission was to disrupt the vital Southern rail system by destroying bridges and disabling equipment. The theft of a locomotive, the *General,* in north Georgia was not their primary objective. (AC)

Stealing the *General*. William Pittenger, a literate member of the raiding party, wrote a detailed, well-illustrated account of the events that transpired during and after the raid behind Confederate lines. His information was mostly accurate but inconsistent, as his book went into three editions. (AC)

Raiders Transported to Knoxville. Nine of the men who were arrested by Confederates for their part in stealing a locomotive were transported to Knoxville for imprisonment and trial. They were famously escorted by members of John Hunt Morgan's band, a group very interested in how men behind enemy lines in civilian clothes would be treated by the justice system. Were they soldiers or spies? (AC)

A Military Court. According to author William Pittenger, the raiders imprisoned in Knoxville were tried separately before a military tribunal in 1862. Several were found guilty and sentenced to hang when a changing military situation in Chattanooga dictated the prisoners be moved to Atlanta so that they could not be liberated by Union troops. (AC)

KNOX COUNTY COURTHOUSE. It was in this building that Andrews' raiders were imprisoned and tried. During their stay, they met David Fry, an East Tennessean who had helped organize the bridge burning in November 1861 and had been captured and jailed. (AC)

DEFENSE ATTORNEY O.P. TEMPLE. Oliver Perry Temple was an active Union leader before the war but had decided not to leave when the Confederates took over. One way he aided the cause was to defend Union soldiers on trial for commando activities. After the war, he wrote about the East Tennessee Civil War experience. (AC)

DEFENSE ATTORNEY JOHN BAXTER. Mostly a Unionist who seemed to change sides a couple of times, Baxter was also an able but unsuccessful defense attorney for Andrews's raiders. After the war, he remained in Knoxville, eventually becoming a US judge. (AC)

THE HANGING OF ANDREWS'S RAIDERS. Ultimately, seven of the captured raiders, along with Andrews who was hanged earlier, were executed in Atlanta. When the graves were moved some years later, it was reported in the popular press that the corpses still wore the nooses that killed him. (AC)

Battle of Fort Donelson. This significant victory for Ulysses S. Grant at Forts Henry and Donelson gave Knoxville its first experience with the death of a well-known son. Young Hugh Lawson McClung, a company captain, died and his body returned to town for burial in Old Gray Cemetery. It was also at this battle that Grant offered his prewar friend Gen. Simon Buckner only unconditional surrender. (LC)

Gen. Edmund Kirby Smith. In October 1862, he was in command of Confederate troops in East Tennessee, based in Knoxville. An invasion of Kentucky, badly coordinated with Gen. Braxton Bragg, produced a Confederate victory at Perryville. Bragg nevertheless ordered a retreat, which caused great anxiety in Knoxville, where the hospitals were filled with additional sick and wounded troops. (LC)

GEN. SAMUEL P. CARTER. In the final days of 1862, native East Tennessean Carter led a cavalry raid into upper East Tennessee. He successfully returned to Kentucky after destroying Rebel property and a railroad bridge but warned that supplying an invasion force over that same terrain would be extremely difficult. This report delayed the advance of Union troops. (SPCL)

COL. WILLIAM P. SANDERS. In June 1863, Sanders and 1,500 mounted troops raced into East Tennessee from Kentucky, staging an artillery barrage against Knoxville. General Buckner was out of town, so wounded soldiers, jailed soldiers, and willing citizens were used to man the defenses. At the conclusion, Sanders sent a note reading, "I send you my compliments and say that but for the admirable manner with which you managed your artillery I would have taken Knoxville today." (AC)

GEN. SIMON BUCKNER. Buckner was in command in Knoxville when the impending Federal invasion of August 1863 was reported. Thinking that Burnside's target would be Chattanooga and the reinforcement of Rosecrans, Buckner was ordered south to reinforce Bragg. On their trip south, the Confederates burned the railroad bridge at Loudon that the Union had been trying to burn for two and a half years. (SPCL)

Five

Federal Occupation

Despite the earnest efforts of Abraham Lincoln to come to the aid of Unionists in East Tennessee, it was not until September 1863 that Federal troops marched south through the mountain passes from Kentucky. The cavalry, including many East Tennesseans who had escaped to Kentucky to enlist in the US Army, was the first unit to enter Knoxville, where throngs of cheering supporters welcomed the return of their native sons. Of course, the fact that many of the Confederate supporters had left with the Confederate army a few days before made it seem as if all of East Tennessee was loyal to the government in Washington, which was far from the case; nevertheless, a long-oppressed populace celebrated Ambrose Burnside's arrival as salvation. The carte de visite collection of the Temple family shows that the arriving Union officers were treated like celebrities.

Native Tennessean general Samuel P. Carter was wisely appointed provost martial, a position for which there was no winning strategy. Animosity toward the recently dominant Rebel population ran high. Unionists looked for restitution for their suffering, while Rebels looked for protection for their families and their property from angry former victims.

William Brownlow returned with the Federals to publish his renamed paper, *The Whig and Rebel Ventilator*. He harbored great anger against his former oppressors, especially against the "she-Rebels," as he tagged the ladies in town, who visibly support the CSA. He was instrumental in having many of these women expelled and also initiating lawsuits against property of absent Confederate leaders.

In late December 1863, Ulysses S. Grant visited Knoxville. A frigid trip north through the Cumberland Gap convinced him that the maintenance of an army in East Tennessee would be almost impossible without a north-south rail line from Kentucky. It was also at this time that priorities shifted, and Sherman's plan to take Atlanta and push deep into the Southern heartland began to take shape. East Tennessee would find itself once again a lawless backwater with insufficient Federal army strength to protect the civilian population.

BURNSIDE'S ARRIVAL IN KNOXVILLE. This iconic *Harper's Weekly* cover depicts Burnside as almost a messianic figure as he arrives on his white horse. Babies held up for his attention and flags, food, and hats in the air all denote the celebration of a long-suffering population. (AC)

GEN. AMBROSE BURNSIDE. This portrait was taken at Schleier's Gallery on Gay Street and is in the Temple family carte de visite collection. Burnside probably had his best military and civilian population experiences of the war here in East Tennessee. He was highly respected by all of his troops, and the Unionist population saw him as a hero. Even the unhappy Confederates did not level much criticism in his direction. (SPCL)

RUGGED MOUNTAIN ORDEAL FOR THE UNION ARMY. Getting over the mountains had been a military concern since the first days of the war when Lincoln tried to get troops into East Tennessee. Hauling artillery, supplies, and men over the severe terrain was arduous; private letters and journals call this march the most grueling advance of the war. (AC)

THE ARRIVAL OF THE RAILROAD IN TOWN. The long hoped for rail connection to Kentucky did not come to Knoxville until 1883. The banner on the engine reads, "First through train to Knoxville." The existence of such a supply route in the 1860s would have changed the entire course of the war for East Tennessee. (SPCL)

Brownlow's Printing Shop. Exiled parson William Brownlow returned with the Union army to immediately resume the publication of his newly renamed newspaper, *The Whig and Rebel Ventilator.* He was welcomed back by Unionists who had stayed, keeping a much lower profile than the parson. (AC)

Refugees in East Tennessee. With the arrival of Federal forces, men who had been hiding out, either deserters or those who had not enlisted at all, came into the liberated territory and offered their services. Burnside's army's strength was greatly increased with the arrival of these new volunteers. (AC)

Rev. Thomas Humes. Minister at St. John's Episcopal Church, Humes had not preached during the Confederate occupation because he refused to pray for Jefferson Davis. A religious man, Burnside installed Reverend Humes back at the pulpit, where he held services for the Union officers. This did not sit well with Confederate parishioners who then had to find a new Sunday morning venue. (MM)

Samuel P. Carter, General and Admiral. Appointed as provost marshal, Carter had a very difficult position. There was simply no way to keep everyone happy and probably no way to keep anyone happy. Rising to the rank of general in the Army, Carter is the only man to also hold the rank of admiral in the Navy. (SPCL)

Maj. Louis Gratz. While popular native son Samuel P. Carter was made the provost marshal, much of the unpleasant administrative business was handled by Major Gratz. Greatly disliked by the Confederate population, he nevertheless married a local girl and settled in Knoxville. Eventually, as a lawyer, he was elected mayor of the newly established North Knoxville. Like so many others in these pages, he is buried in Old Gray Cemetery. (MHC)

GEN. ULYSSES S. GRANT. This carte de visite is in the Temple family collection. In late December 1863, Grant came to Knoxville to inspect the area firsthand. The harsh winter climate and an arduous trip back to Kentucky through the Cumberland Gap impressed him strongly as to the difficulties of supplying an army in East Tennessee. He was also in contact with his friend William T. Sherman, and as their new plans took shape, upper East Tennessee was again abandoned to want and lawlessness. (SPCL)

A RIVERBOAT ON THE TENNESSEE RIVER. Knoxville's location on the Holston River meant that some supplies could be sent by water up from Chattanooga. Without a rail line over the mountains through the Cumberland Gap, a line that did not exist during the war, supplies from the North had to come from Nashville, to Chattanooga, and then to Knoxville. The Cumberland Plateau was too great an obstacle for engineers to tackle during the war. (SPCL)

Gen. William T. Sherman. Sherman's plan for victory had great impact on the fate of East Tennessee. He personally had little regard for the area, and militarily his reasoning was probably sound. After racing to aid Burnside, he could not wait to get back to Chattanooga, apparently unconcerned about following Longstreet into upper East Tennessee. He did, however, visit at least once more in March 1864 when he requested and received the transfers of Poe and Barnard. (LC)

Gen. Philip Sheridan. Sheridan accompanied Sherman to Knoxville in December 1863 and is reputed to have enjoyed his command in the area. This carte de visite is also in the Temple collection. Sheridan was erroneously reported in some private correspondence to be engaged to a Knoxville girl. (SPCL)

GEN. JOHN FOSTER. Mainly for health reasons, Burnside had asked to be replaced as commander in Knoxville. Ready to take over the job, Gen. John Foster arrived in early December of 1863. In bad health, he had time enough in town to oversee one of the most unfortunate incidents of a time of highly charged emotions just after the retreat of Longstreet's army: the case of Ephraim S. Dodd. (LC)

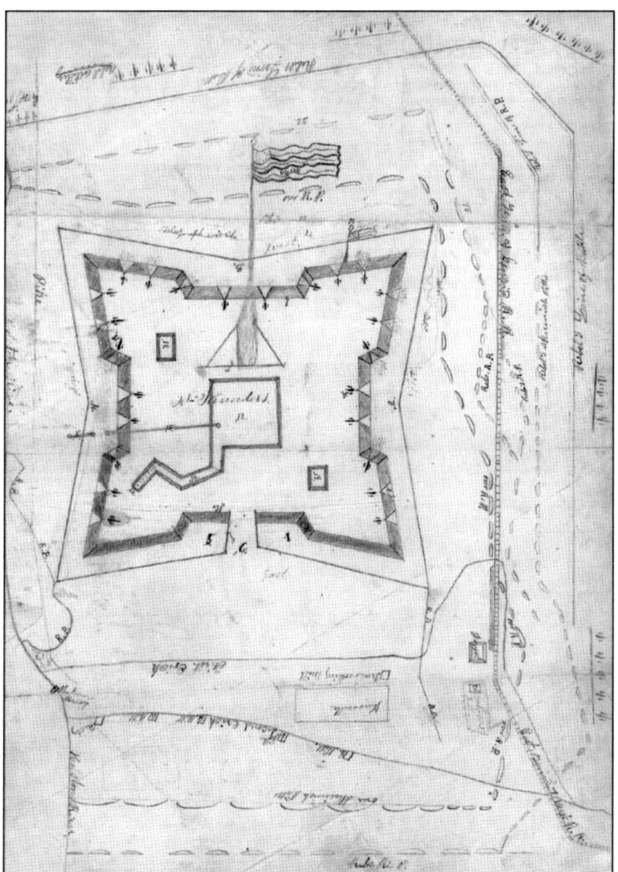

FORT SANDERS WITH FOUR BASTIONS COMPLETED. This hand-drawn map by John Orth includes details unavailable on many of the more professional versions. For one thing, the story of Dodd's hanging leads to the location of the gallows somewhere near present-day Henley Street and the railroad tracks. The handwritten legend on this map of Fort Sanders documents the event. (LC)

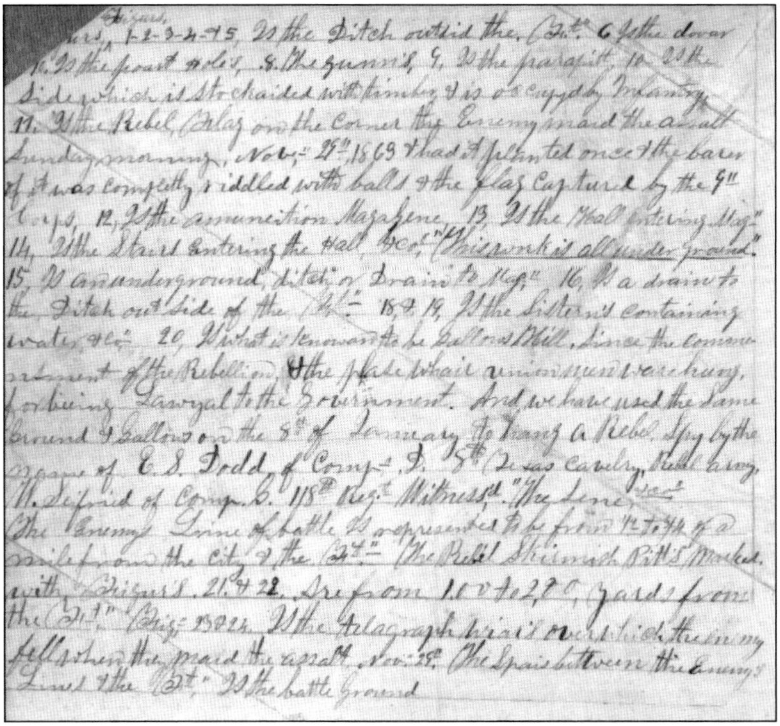

Figures, [illegible], 1-2-3-4-&5, Is the Ditch outsid the Ft. 6 Is the door
7. Is the frost holes, 8. The gunns, 9. Is the parapitt, 10 Is the
Side which is Stockaided with timber & is occupyd by Infantry
11. Is the Rebel Flag on the Corner they Enemy maid the assalt
Sunday morning, Nov. 29th 1863 & had it planted once & the bars
of it was compleatly riddled with balls & the flag Captured by the 9th
Corps, 12, Is the ammunition Magazene 13, Is the Hall entering Mag.
14, Is the Stairs entering the Hall &c. (This work is all under ground.
15, Is an underground ditch or Drain to Mag. 16, Is a drain to
the Ditch outside of the Ft. 18 & 19, Is the Sisterns Containing
water &c. 20, Is what is known to be Gallows Hill, Since the comme-
ncement of the Rebellion, & the place whare union men ware hung,
for being Loyal to the Government. And we have used the Same
Ground & Gallows on the 8th of January to hang a Rebel Spy by the
name of E. S. Dodd of Comp. D. 8th Texas Cavelry, Rebel army.
M. Seifried of Comp. C. 118th Reg. Witnessed. The Line &c.
The Enemys Line of battle is represented to be from 1/2 to 3/4 of a
mile from the City & the Ft. The Rebel Skirmish Pitts Marked
with Figure's 21 & 22. Are from 100 to 200 yards from
the Ft. [illegible] 23 & 24 Is the telegraph wire over which the enemy
fell when they maid the assalt Nov. 29. The Space between the enemys
Line & the Ft. Is the battle Ground

The Hanging of Texas Ranger E.S. Dodd. A young cavalry soldier with Terry's Texas Rangers, Dodd was arrested when he was caught behind Union lines south of the river. Wearing a stolen Union overcoat and carrying an ambiguous diary led to charges of spying, and Foster's orders were clear. This was a sad act of vengeance; the community wanted to see a Rebel die on the same gallows used to hang Unionists. (LC)

Gravestone for E.S. Dodd. While no one knows exactly where Dodd was buried, he is still entitled to an official military tombstone. This stone with no body commemorates the sad story and sits in the garden outside Confederate Memorial Hall on Kingston Pike. Also known as Bleak House, the home is open to the public. (AC)

GEN. DAVIS TILLSON. In command in Knoxville during the winter of 1864, he enlarged and redesigned some of Poe's earthworks. Poe was not especially pleased with the changes he saw in March 1864. Tillson also changed the names of some of the forts and batteries that had been officially designated by Burnside. Losing a foot while a cadet at West Point did not seem to derail Tillson's military career. (SPCL)

GEN. JOHN SCHOFIELD AND STAFF. Schofield later gained fame because of his victory at the Battle of Franklin in 1864. His decimation of Hood's army and the subsequent battle of Nashville ended any further Southern hope of retaking territory in Tennessee or north of it. This card is also in the Temple carte de visite collection. (SPCL)

Military Bridge Completed. The military did provide Knoxville with at least one civic improvement. The sturdy new bridge, built with stone piers quarried from the south side of the river, provided a permanent link between the north and south sides of the river until a flood destroyed it a couple of years later. (MM)

Ruins of a Home in Strawberry Plains. Union forces never did totally control upper East Tennessee. Violence continued just beyond the reach of troops based in Knoxville. Longstreet's army wintered in Russellville, foraging for all they needed and driving the destitute civilian population out of their homes. Many became refugees in Knoxville, where severe food shortages, epidemics, and lack of housing made for desperate times. There was also a growing freedman population in need of help. (LC)

Edward Everett. This philanthropist from Massachusetts, informed of the desperate condition of the people of East Tennessee, worked with Rev. Thomas Humes to secure aid from the Northeast. Over $100,000 in contributions was converted to supplies going directly to the suffering population in the area. As a side note of history, it was Everett who spoke in Gettysburg just before Lincoln's famous address. He later wrote to Lincoln, "I would be glad, if I could flatter myself that I came as near to the central idea of the occasion, in two hours, as you did in two minutes." (AC)

General George Stoneman. In 1864, from his base in Knoxville, Stoneman made a raid on Saltville, Virginia, destroying the Confederates' ability to use the site for salt production. Interestingly, it was the McClung family of Knoxville who had the salt contract for the state of Tennessee. (SPCL)

Sgt. Edward and Nannie Kline. Possibly taken on their wedding day, this is the only currently known image of a member of the US Colored Troops 1st Heavy Artillery. This regiment was raised in Knoxville in the early months of 1864; Kline was in Company E. The original Kline family home, where eight slaves were owned in 1860, still stands on Bell Road south of Loudon. (Courtesy of Gerald Augustus.)

Six

Knoxville, a Proud City

The city of Knoxville was justifiably proud of itself in 1861. Since its founding in 1792, it had grown into the largest town in the region with impressive public buildings, a planned downtown, river transport, decent roads, fine homes, a respected university, and developing cultural institutions. The recent completion of the railroad from Virginia to Georgia contributed to the increased growth and prosperity in a place that had already established itself as a regional trade and distribution center.

It was this same position on the vital single-gauge link between the armies of Gen. Robert E. Lee around Richmond and the troops and ordnance from the Deep South that made Knoxville strategically of the first order to the Confederate military. From the earliest days of the war, troop trains came through town carrying rowdy and eager young volunteers whose patriotic zeal sometimes spilled over into the streets of Knoxville.

By the middle of the war, the effects of two years of military occupation were evident. All elements of the infrastructure of the town had been badly damaged by troops of both sides. There was not a chicken coop or fence to be found. Lawns were gone, confiscated home were in disrepair, and all the churches except St. John's were used as barracks or hospitals. Homes and the railroad facility were burned during the siege of Knoxville; with the Union occupation, the housing and feeding needs of thousands of extra men, horses, and mules continued to take their toll. Diseases like small pox reached epidemic proportions.

The arrival of the Federals initially brought the hope of recovery, but the relegation of the town to secondary importance in the Union's plan for military victory allowed the distress to worsen, as a burgeoning refugee crisis created a whole new level of community suffering.

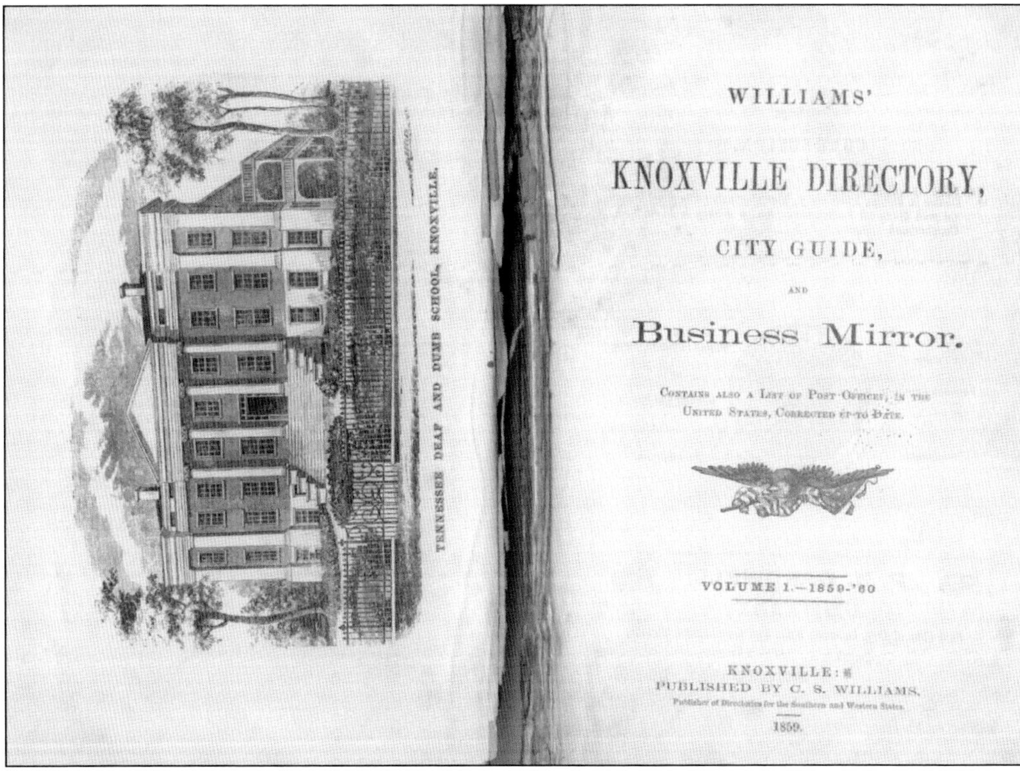
TENNESSEE DEAF AND DUMB SCHOOL, KNOXVILLE.

WILLIAMS'

KNOXVILLE DIRECTORY,

CITY GUIDE,

AND

Business Mirror.

Contains also a List of Post-Offices, in the United States, Corrected up-to Date.

VOLUME 1.—1859-'60

KNOXVILLE:

PUBLISHED BY C. S. WILLIAMS,

Publisher of Directories for the Southern and Western States.

1859.

WILLIAMS'S KNOXVILLE CITY DIRECTORY, 1859–1860. As war loomed on the national horizon, business was growing in "the heart of the valley." The city's business, banking, and professional leaders, who went on to play major community, and for some national, roles in the war that would arrive in less than a year, can all be found in this small but respectable volume. (SPCL)

MAYOR JAMES CHURCHWELL LUTTRELL. Surprisingly, this man, with his roots in Knoxville, was mayor when the war began, mayor all through the war, and mayor when it was over. He must have been an extraordinary politician. His sons fought on opposite sides during the war, but upon their return both subsequently became mayors of the town in the later 1800s. (MHC)

SCHLEIER PANORAMA OF KNOXVILLE, 1866. Taken from the heights south of the river looking north, many details of the town are evident in this four-frame panorama. Note the university buildings on the hill, Fort Sanders on the top of the ridge behind the university, a military encampment to the right of the university, and the piers for the still unfinished railroad bridge in the river. (MM)

FROM SOUTH OF THE RIVER, FRAME NO. 2. In this frame, the Dickinson house on the right is the most prominent structure. Beside it to the right is most of Castle Fox, the nickname of the county jail. One local historian identified the tree in front of Dickinson's house as the one on which a Confederate veteran was hanged by a mob in April 1865. Proximity to the jail certainly makes that possible. Note the wash on the line and the shadows indicating the sun was in the west. (MM)

From South of the River, Frame No. 3. The pillars of First Presbyterian Church stand out against the surrounding trees on the far right. The white tower of the courthouse is in the center of the image. The spires of the Second Presbyterian Church and Methodist church rise in the upper left. Just to the right of Second Presbyterian is the distinctive building on Market Square. The small cabins in the foreground may be part of the elusive freedmen's village. (MM)

From South of the River, Frame No. 4. Note the completed military bridge spanning the river. The long buildings on the right housed a facility for raising and processing hogs. The white fence (right center) on Methodist Hill was probably used for prisoners during the war. A white covered bridge crosses over First Creek at Clinch Avenue toward the left center. (MM)

FROM SOUTH OF THE RIVER. In this seldom-seen view, details of the Knox County Jail, not visible in the four-frame panorama, can be discerned. The unusual architecture and its location among the best homes of the city are more apparent in this rendering from Fort Stanley back toward the town. (MM)

RIVER TRANSPORT. This photograph, taken after the war, shows a severely overloaded riverboat named *City of Knoxville* (visible on the side) filled civilian passengers. In 1864–1865, supplies from Chattanooga were shipped in similar vessels to attempt to keep the full garrison in Knoxville fed, clothed, and armed. Sustaining an army in East Tennessee never ceased to be difficult. (SPCL)

DEAF AND DUMB ASYLUM. Opened in 1848, when the Civil War began this facility was immediately filled with young men who were victims of the diseases prevalent in the military training camps all around town. It continued to be used in this capacity throughout the war. On the town's northern defensive line, it was not turned into a fort or battery. Note the soldiers on the roof; black sashes may indicate this photograph was taken after Lincoln's assassination. (MHC)

EAST TENNESSEE UNIVERSITY. The university was closed during the war, as the instructors and all male students made their personal decisions about which side to fight for. The buildings saw combat and were heavily shelled just before the Battle of Fort Sanders. After the war, Rev. Thomas Humes was appointed as the new president. Damaged buildings could not be immediately reoccupied, and students helped refurbish the facility and plant new trees on the stripped campus. (MM)

The Knox County Courthouse. Built in 1850, this imposing structure endured many wartime activities. It was located on Main Street across the street from what is now called "the old courthouse." This building and the jail down the street were so overcrowded that a house on the corner of Main and Prince (now Market) Streets, along with a large building on Methodist Hill in East Knoxville, were also used as prisons. (MM)

The Female Institute. Long ago located at present-day Henley and Main Streets, this venerable institution was where all the daughters of the first families of Knoxville went to receive their education. While normally above reproach, it once had to defend charges of being too liberal. It was also closed to students during the war. (MM)

PARK HOUSE. This fine home still stands, beautifully renovated, across from St. John's Cathedral. Construction is reputed to have been started by Gov. John Sevier, but by 1812 the Park family lived here and continued to do so for the next 100 years. Living across the street from Unionist Thomas Humes, the Parks were Confederates during the war as were their other neighbors, the Frank McClungs. (MM)

DICKINSON HOUSE. Perez Dickinson and his family moved to Knoxville from Massachusetts so that he could teach at the university. It did not take him too long to discover that he could make more money as a merchant, so he went into business with his brother-in-law James Cowan, a Knoxville native. He left town for the first part of the war after being fined for probably being a Unionist. Situated next to the jail, it was probably on his property that a young Confederate veteran was hanged by a mob in 1865. (MM)

Blount Mansion. Built in the 1790s, the governor's house was occupied by the Boyd family during the Civil War. Despite the fact that the oldest son was a surgeon in the Confederate army, the ladies entertained officers of both sides with musical evenings at the home and riding parties into the country. In the spring of 1862, cousin Belle Boyd, already a famous Rebel spy, praised the gaiety of the town during her stay with her relatives. The home is open to the public. (MM)

Bleak House. Now also known as Confederate Hall and owned by Chapter 89 of the United Daughters of the Confederacy, this fine home was Longstreet's headquarters during the siege of Knoxville. It still exhibits damage caused by artillery fire. The tower has a drawing of three young sharpshooters supposedly killed by shell fire from Fort Sanders. Tours of the home are available. (AC)

Crozier Mansion. The well-appointed home of Confederate John Crozier, this house sat well back from the street on the corner of Gay and Clinch Streets. Ambrose Burnside chose it for his headquarters. From here, he was in telegraph communication with his entire defensive line during the siege thanks to the talents of Orlando Poe. The house was demolished to build the Farragut Hotel. (AC)

Brownlow House. William and Eliza Brownlow lived modestly with their seven children in this East Knoxville home. It became something of a tourist attraction for visitors to the town during Union occupation. The site was consumed by urban renewal in the mid-20th century. (MM)

Ramsey House. This is Swan Pond, the home owned by Dr. J.G.M. Ramsey's father, Francis A. Ramsey. The doctor's own home, called Mecklenburg, was burned during the first week of Federal occupation. It was located at the fork where the Holston and French Broad Rivers come together. An active Confederate leader, Ramsey openly blamed William Brownlow for hiring some lowly soldier to torch the home, which contained an irreplaceable library of Tennessee history. This home is open to the public. (LC)

Mabry-Hazen House. On a hill on the far east side of Knoxville, the grounds of this home were fortified throughout the war. Laura Mabry, who lived here with her husband and many children, did this sketch of her lovely home with earthworks all around. This well-preserved home is still standing, practically unchanged in 150 years, and is open to the public. (Courtesy of Mabry-Hazen Foundation.)

First Presbyterian Church. James White, Knoxville's earliest settler, donated the land for this first church in Knoxville; the name Church Street was given to the street upon which it sits. Used as a hospital and perhaps barracks during the war, it was only after the war that the congregation was allowed to take possession again. The cemetery contains the grave of Abner Baker, the young Confederate veteran hanged by a mob in 1865. (MM)

Second Presbyterian Church. This beautiful new church building opened in 1860. The cemetery in which Gen. William Sanders was buried is on the right. The congregation was very much pro-Confederate in 1861, even though Horace Maynard, elected to the US Congress during the war, was a member. The site was sold in the 1890s, and the cemetery was moved. (MM)

Immaculate Conception Catholic Church. On a ridgetop with a commanding view, this church is on the northern line of defense. Battery Wiltsie was built beside it. The first church on the site faced west; the newer, larger, present-day church faces north. At the close of the war, Fr. Abram Ryan, called the "Poet Priest of the Confederacy," was a priest here. (MM)

St. John's Episcopal Church. A Unionist minister, a Confederate congregation, and a central location ensured that this church would play a key role in the story of the war in Knoxville. It was the only church not closed by the Federals and put to other uses. After Federal occupation, Rev. Thomas Humes organized a school to teach freedmen to read and write. (MM)

METHODIST CHURCH. Sitting on Temperance Hill in East Knoxville, this small church was aligned with the Union cause and Methodist parson William Brownlow. It was in this neighborhood that the May 1861 pro-Union convention took place. (MM)

SKETCH OF KNOXVILLE, 1863. Recently acquired by the Calvin M. McClung Historical Collection, this charcoal sketch of Knoxville appears to have been created just after the Federal occupation. The artist looks across Second Creek to a town covered with tents and military presence. Details of church spires, street layout, and smokestacks all enrich the knowledge of this town as it existed at an important juncture in the war. (MHC)

Seven

FAMILIES

When war came to Knoxville, the civilian population was no more prepared to handle it than any other American community; perhaps it was less so since this population was almost equally divided in its sympathies to one side or the other. There was no one position buoying the civilian population on the home front. The community respect and support of the families left behind by the departure of men to fight was absent, as those families left behind knew their loved ones could be somewhere killing each other. Encountering lifelong friends on the street who could now be termed the enemy was devastating for those who had to experience such interaction on a daily basis.

For the first half of the war, the Confederate civilian population was dominant over the Unionists who remained. In September 1863, the roles were reversed. The faces and stories of the individuals who lived through this punishing time are poignant. There was no code of behavior available about how to cope with this extreme social order. The community had to find the answers within themselves. Like people everywhere, some lived and died with honor, while others gave into baser instincts of greed and self-preservation.

Leading families are the ones whose legacies have been preserved because of their ability to record their images with the new medium of photography. Those not wealthy enough to capture their images or lucky enough to have their letters survive, or who were illiterate, may exist only as printed names on an enlistment roster or census sheet; so many stories have been lost to time.

Regrettably, finding material on the African American experience during and after the war is very difficult. After surviving the war and gaining citizenship, the freedmen of Knoxville waged a hard-fought struggle to create a viable community. Perhaps more research and some luck will reveal details of the challenges and successes.

Dr. James Gettys McGready Ramsey. A medical doctor, financier, historian, and a civic activist, Ramsey was 62 when the war broke out. He nevertheless volunteered for service, as did five of his sons. The parents of 14 children, he and his wife, Margaret Crozier Ramsey, devoted everything to the Southern cause. One son died of wounds received in combat, and the deaths of two daughters were war related. (MHC)

Henrietta Ramsey Lenoir. Dr. J.G.M. Ramsey's daughter, she was the wife of Dr. Benjamin Lenoir of Lenoir Station. She personally encountered General Sanders during his raid in June 1863 and declared him to be a gentleman. After the Union took over, her husband was jailed for a time. Then, her two small sons contracted a disease (maybe scarlet fever or diphtheria) and died on the same day. She never got over her grief and died in 1864. (Courtesy of Loudon County Historical Society.)

Parson William Gannaway Brownlow. If Dr. Ramsey can be said to represent the extreme Confederate stance, Brownlow can play the same role for the Union. The father of seven, he had two sons in the Union cavalry. He and his wife, Eliza, and daughters were evicted from Knoxville, later returning with the Union army. The postwar governor of Tennessee, he neither forgot nor forgave the treatment he had received from former Confederates. (AC)

Eliza O'Brien Brownlow. Eliza Brownlow kept a low profile, but having a larger-than-life husband, perhaps that was inevitable. She was loyal to the Union cause, but her brother fought for a Louisiana regiment. He was wounded in the Battle of Fort Sanders and recuperated at her home. She was the mother of seven children; her two sons served as Union cavalry officers. (SPCL)

GEN. JAMES P. BROWNLOW. Colonel of the 1st Tennessee Volunteer Cavalry, he had a distinguished cavalry career and was noted for his daring and unconventionality. Never totally recovering from his war wounds, he died in 1879. He was the son of William and Eliza. His brother John was also a Federal cavalry colonel. (MHC)

SUSAN BROWNLOW. The daughter of William and Eliza, who was also called Martha and Maud in Northern publications, Susan famously defended flying the US flag in front of her home, challenging the threats of CSA soldiers to pull it down. She accompanied her father on his lecture tour in the North and was something of a celebrity in her own right. (MHC)

Louise Franklin Armstrong. The wife of Robert and sister-in-law of John Mason Boyd, as well as numerous other kinship connections with prominent Knoxville families, Louise sat upstairs in a bedroom with her small children during the siege and Battle of Fort Sanders. Her home, Bleak House, was Longstreet's headquarters and suffered direct cannon fire. She famously entertained Longstreet and the returning members of the 79th Highlanders at the Blue and Gray Reunion of 1890. (MHC)

Dr. John Mason Boyd. Left in charge when his father Judge Samuel Beckett Boyd died in 1858, he supported his mother and seven younger siblings. When the war broke out, he joined the CSA as a surgeon tending the wounded at the first Battle of Bull Run. John and his younger brother Samuel (married to the sister of Louise Armstrong) practiced medicine in Knoxville for many years and were highly respected by the community. (MM)

Boyd Family Portrait. Dr. John Mason Boyd stands behind his mother and seven younger siblings, a musical family. Sue sits to the left of her mother. Their home in Blount Mansion was a social center throughout the war as they entertained CSA and Union officers alike. In the 1890s, Sue told a newspaper reporter about a riding party on the day Sanders was killed and singing "The Valley of Chamonix" from sheet music he provided. (MHC)

Susan Boyd Barton. A lifelong resident of Knoxville, Sue figures prominently in the letters of Orlando Poe. He wrote that Sue believed she was being courted by Doc Sanders, but Poe commented that he knew differently and was amazed how young women could deceive themselves. The whole story is lost to time since Sanders died in November 1863 with no surviving letters or diaries. (MHC)

Belle Boyd. Belle was already quite famous when, in the early months of 1863, her mentor Gen. Stonewall Jackson advised her to go to visit her relatives in Tennessee. He wrote she would be imprisoned again if she tried to return to her home in Virginia, then under Federal control. She took his advice and visited her aunt Susan in Knoxville at Blount Mansion. In her autobiography, she wrote of her reception by a military brass band and many pleasant social activities. (LC)

Margaret Christian Russell Cowan Humes Ramsey. Through this lovely lady, most of Knoxville became related. She was married three times, and each time her husband died while she was pregnant. Three sons were born under those conditions, with seven sons total. Sons Unionist Thomas Humes and Confederate J.G.M. Ramsey were step brothers. (MHC)

Horace Maynard. Hailing from Massachusetts, Horace moved to Knoxville in 1837. Originally an educator, he became a lawyer and then went into politics. Initially opposed to the institution of slavery, he became a slave owner but was nevertheless very much a Unionist, who went to Washington as an elected representative from a Southern state during the war. He was a tireless advocate for the military invasion of East Tennessee and found Lincoln to be a strong supporter. (SPCL)

Edward or Washburn Maynard. Both of Horace Maynard's sons joined the Union cavalry. This image was with that of the elder Maynard in the carte de visite collection of the Temple family. Both sons returned from the war: Edward died in Foreign Service in 1868, and Washburn became a rear admiral in the US Navy. (SPCL)

METHODIST MINISTER DAVID SULLINS. In 1861, Reverend Sullins joined the Mabry Grays as a chaplain. His church, in fact the majority of the churches in Knoxville, was pro-Confederacy. The church itself was across the street from the Second Presbyterian Church, near Market Square, during the war. (MHC)

ELIZA MORGAN MCCLUNG. The widow of Matthew McClung and the mother of 10 children, she was one of the wealthiest people in town in 1861. Her youngest son, Hugh, was eager to enlist and died fighting for the Confederacy in the Battle of Fort Donelson shortly after his 23rd birthday. Eliza was wealthy enough to leave town and spent some of the war in Sing Sing (Ossining), New York. (MM)

Ellen McClung Marshall. Eliza's youngest daughter, Ellen McClung Marshall and her mother are often mentioned in the diary of Ellen Renshaw House. All the McClungs supported the Confederacy, and she helped secure food and clothing for CSA casualties housed in Knoxville jails and hospitals. She married shortly after the war, but unfortunately her husband was killed in an 1871 train crash near Nashville. (MM)

Hugh Lawson McClung. Eliza's youngest son, Hugh, was a college student who hoped to go on to Princeton University. His mother wanted him to come home and work for the family business for a while. When the war broke out, all plans for the future were forever altered. He died as a company captain at the Battle of Fort Donelson in early 1862. His body was shipped back to Knoxville for burial in Old Gray Cemetery, the first member of a prominent local family to die in the war. (MM)

FRANKLIN H. MCCLUNG. The museum at the University of Tennessee was created in Franklin H. McClung's memory by his daughter Ellen McClung Green. His activities during the war are somewhat vague; his obituary makes no mention of it. He was probably at the attack on Knoxville in 1863, in which his cousin Pleasant was killed, but the report in the newspaper thanking many also says many more were there who did not want their names published. He later worked on salt production in Saltville, Virginia. (MM)

ELIZA MILLS MCCLUNG, WIFE OF FRANK. From a prominent St. Louis family, Eliza was the mother of 10 children. She and the children lived in their home across from St. John's Church for much of the war, but letters from St. Louis indicate that she was allowed to travel. Her home was in danger of being confiscated as Rebel property, but knowing many lawyers seems to have influenced the process. During Union occupation, she did have Union officers staying in her large house. (MM)

MATHILDA MCCLUNG. Young Tilly McClung left a Civil War story. In the early 1900s, a brother who never knew her wrote to a General Fitzgerald in New York. He was sending a photograph taken of the officer and young Tilly during "your stay at our father's home." The general wrote back thanking the brother for the photograph, fondly remembering the occasion. Now lost, the image of Tilly and the officer would have been taken at roughly the same time as the one seen here. Tilly died in 1873, possibly during the cholera outbreak that year. (MM)

COL. FRANCIS MARION GREEN. From Oxford, Mississippi, Colonel Green left a young wife and two small sons when he went off to fight for the Confederacy. He was killed at the Battle of Spotsylvania and buried in Virginia. In the 1930s, Francis's son John, who had never known his father and later became a judge in Knoxville, made a pilgrimage to his father's grave and returned with haunting photographs (see page 120). Judge Green wrote later about the war, stating he would have fought for the Confederacy but that the war never should have happened. (MM)

Elliot Spotswood McClung. From Huntsville, Alabama, "Cousin Spot" and his brother Hugh Lawson White McClung (one of four Hugh McClung's in town at the time) came to Knoxville to raise McClung's Battery in 1861. Despite being dishonorably discharged from the Confederate army for issues involving payroll in 1863, Spot reenlisted and continued to fight. After capture and serving time in a Union prison, he settled in Knoxville and ran a successful hauling business. (MM)

Laura and Joseph Mabry. Joseph was the largest slaveholder in Knox County and already a wealthy man when war broke out. He outfitted the Mabry Grays and was called "General" from then on for his efforts. He then made a profit selling diverse materials to the Confederate army, but when the Federals arrived he quickly took the oath and sold more supplies to them. The couple had 14 children, only 6 of whom lived to adulthood. He and his oldest son were famously gunned down on Gay Street in 1881. (Courtesy of Mabry-Hazen Foundation.)

George Washington Mabry. Brother of Joseph, this charming portrait is of George and his grandson after the war. During the war, he stayed on his large farm west of town, a reluctant Confederate who probably purchased a substitute for his military service. His wife, Jeanette Hume Mabry, was the sister of Mrs. Oliver P. Temple and an outspoken Unionist. (MHC)

Belle Mabry. There is no record of the sympathies of Belle, the daughter of George and Jeanette Mabry, but it could not have been easy living in a divided home. She was the cousin of O.P. Temple's daughter Mary Boyce Temple, to whom this carte de visite is inscribed. It is part of the Temple carte de visite collection. (SPCL)

Duff Green Thornburgh. The Thornburghs of New Market were staunch and active Union supporters. One member of the family was sent to prison in Tuscaloosa and died there. Four younger men—Duff, John, Russell, and Jacob—were all cavalry officers. Duff went to Washington, DC, to work in the post office after the war but is buried in Old Gray Cemetery. (MM)

Ellen Renshaw House. Ellen was 19 in 1863 when she began keeping a diary so she could preserve all the details of her wartime experiences for her younger brother John, who was serving in the Confederate army. A self-described "very violent Rebel," her writing captures details of events, people, and places that greatly enhance today's understanding of the lives of civilians during the war, which otherwise would have been lost to time. (Courtesy of the House family.)

Eight
Memory

History, tradition, family, religion, and kinship are all of highest importance to the people of East Tennessee. Yet, the four years between 1861 and 1865 have left almost no imprint on the cultural identity of Knoxville and the surrounding area. At first, it might seem that is because nothing much happened in town. In fact, everything horrible about war did happen here, not just to soldiers but also to the civilian population. For the community, the only way to endure the peace, to let go of the animosity and hatred bred by war, was to leave it in the past. No prominent streets, buildings, or schools are named for Civil War heroes. No annual holiday commemorates the time. Even most historical markers are badly placed for public consumption. For many families, the stories were rarely told and questions seldom answered. The "recent unpleasantness" had to be abandoned for future success.

Nevertheless, in obscure parts of town, monuments do exist. On busy thoroughfares, other memorials hide in plain sight. Cemeteries tell their own stories of the lives of those who suffered through that punishing time, and despite almost no conscious effort to preserve "the scars of war," in fact in secluded places the fortifications can still be found.

Maps, official reports, county records, photographs, and personal accounts are excellent ways to learn the content of the past. But the artifacts and the places of that past that have survived despite a conscious effort to forget are of intrinsic value. Standing on the hallowed ground of a long forgotten battle, climbing the bastion of a neglected fort, and viewing the panorama today geographically unchanged in 150 years are powerful experiences, and they reinforce the fact that where history happened is important.

With this sesquicentennial of the Civil War, Knox County has acknowledged the power of its past and begun the excavation and exhibition of it for residents and for the thousands of descendants of the men from every state in the Union and the Confederacy who lived, died, camped, or fought in this forgotten theater of war. It is a mission to restore the past to its rightful place in the cultural identity of East Tennessee and the nation.

Jewish Confederates. The first Jewish cemetery in Knoxville was established in part to accommodate the bodies of two young soldiers who died, probably of disease, in Virginia and whose bodies were sent back south on the railroad. Genealogical research has shown that the date of birth on this stone is incorrect, but the name and date of death are accurate. (AC)

Confederate Monument in Bethel Cemetery. In 1891, the Ladies Memorial Society had finally raised enough money to erect this impressive memorial. The statue on the top is of a Confederate soldier and was sculpted by Knoxville artist Lloyd Branson. The cemetery is part of the Mabry-Hazen property and is open to the public. (MM)

Knoxville National Cemetery. This cemetery was established by General Burnside for the Union soldiers killed here, beginning in 1863. This print shows the graves of members of the 79th Highlanders Regiment who served inside Fort Sanders at the time of the battle. The names and dates of death of actual soldiers can be read on the stones depicted here. For many years, it was the largest Union cemetery in the South. (LC)

Union Monument with Eagle. In 1901, about 10 years after the installation of the Confederate monument, this memorial was built in the National Cemetery by donations of Union supporters. Only three years after it was erected, the brass eagle was struck by lightning, destroying much of the monument and sending the eagle out into the street. (AC)

UNION MONUMENT WITH SOLDIER. When the Union memorial was repaired, a stone soldier was installed in place of the brass eagle. Legend has it that it was purposely made just a bit taller than the Confederate statue across town. In 2009, it was totally refurbished. Its castle-like architecture enshrines engraved statistics on the number of men from Tennessee who fought for the Union. (AC)

UNITED DAUGHTERS OF THE CONFEDERACY MEMORIAL. In 1914, Chapter 89 of the United Daughters of the Confederacy installed this marble monument on the top of the hill at Seventeenth and Laurel Streets where the attack of November 29, 1863, took place. Unfortunately, Seventeenth Street is now so busy it is difficult to park and inspect the stone up close. (AC)

79TH NEW YORK HIGHLANDERS REGIMENTAL MEMORIAL. In 1918, members of the regiment had this monument of their time in Knoxville installed near where they were camped during the siege and battle. It is the only such monument in Knoxville, and very few people have any idea why it sits at the corner of Sixteenth Street and White Avenue. (Courtesy of Stephanie Drumheller-Horton.)

MEMORIAL TO A BELOVED PHYSICIAN. Dr. John Mason Boyd's memorial was erected on the courthouse lawn and was paid for by donations by the people of Knoxville. Dr. Boyd had served in the Confederate army and was actually present at the first battle at Manassas (Bull Run). He is one example of a man who returned to Knoxville after the war, resumed his career, and became a pillar of the community. (MHC)

THE *SULTANA* DISASTER. Despite the fact that more people died in this maritime disaster than on the *Titanic*, very few people have ever heard the story. On April 27, 1865, the war was over, Lincoln had just been assassinated, and Union survivors of prison camps in Andersonville and Cahaba were finally returning home on a dangerously overloaded riverboat on the Mississippi River near Memphis. (LC)

A *SULTANA* SURVIVOR. This young boy had been a soldier, a prisoner of war, and finally a survivor of the fiery explosion that sank the riverboat, bringing him and some 2,200 others home. Of that total, some 1,700 (the exact number will never be known) died of concussion, fire, or drowning. (Courtesy of Tennessee State Library and Archives.)

A Forgotten Memorial. In the early 1900s, a memorial was erected in Mount Olive Cemetery for the victims of the *Sultana*. The number of men from each state and their names are engraved in stone. Reunions of the survivors were held here for many years. (Courtesy of Tennessee State Library and Archives.)

Confederate Soldier on a Veteran's Grave. This nearly life-size statue of a Confederate soldier adorns a grave in Old Gray Cemetery. While most people left no trace as to their leanings during the Civil War at their gravesites in Knoxville's historic cemetery, a few made every effort to memorialize their roles. (AU)

A Grave Far from Home. Many soldiers, even officers, were buried in a distant location. The fortunate were identified, and in this unusual instance a headstone was erected. Col. Francis Marion Green of Oxford, Mississippi, was killed at the Battle of Spotsylvania. In the 1930s, his son Judge John Green, who was married to Frank H. McClung's daughter, made a pilgrimage north to visit his father's grave and returned with this photograph. (MM)

Natural Erosion Melting Away History. This picture, taken in the 1880s, shows the erosion of the earthworks that made up Fort Sanders. Large homes were being built on this prime real estate, and despite the occasional appeal for preservation of the site, no serious opposition appeared to deflect development. Today, the fort at Seventeenth and Laurel Streets is completely obliterated. (SPCL)

The Chamber of Commerce Brochure. In 1890, Knoxville was all about development and looking to the future. This brochure printed for veterans barely mentions the war, and there is no map showing where anything of military significance took place. It emphasizes the opportunities available in Knoxville and its recent accomplishments. "Progress" was the watchword of the day. (AC)

Blue and Gray Reunion. In 1890, a huge tent could not contain all of the 10,000 veterans who returned to Knoxville to celebrate their experiences 27 years earlier as deadly foes. There were parades, speeches, dinners, athletic competitions, and a spectacular fireworks display. Commitment to a shared future was the dominant theme. (MM)

ITS MEMORY ALONE REMAINS. This commemorative medal was designed for the 1890 reunion. One side of it shows a Confederate and a Union soldier shaking hands, while the reverse depicts the northwest bastion at the Battle of Fort Sanders and proclaims, "Its memory alone remains." (AC)

JAMES LONGSTREET. The famous general returned to Knoxville in 1890 for the Blue and Gray Reunion. Wounded in the throat during the Battle of the Wilderness, his speech was read for him. He paid a visit to the charming Louise Armstrong at Bleak House, where he presented her with a sword. Longstreet was then made an honorary member of the 79th Highlanders Regiment. (LC)

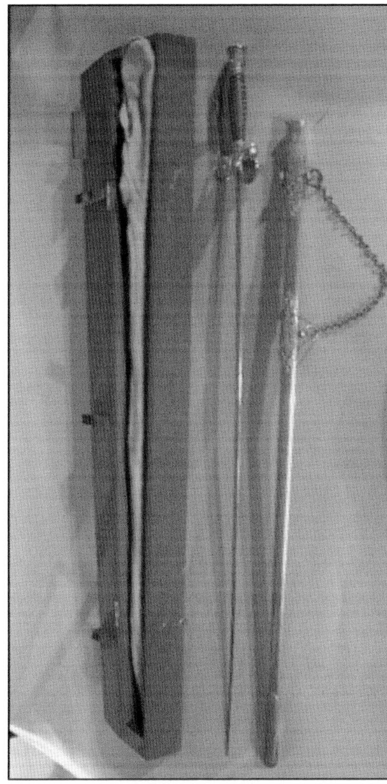

Orville E. Babcock's Sword. After the Knoxville Campaign, Gen. Orville Babcock joined General Grant's staff and was present at the surrender at Appomattox. In fact, he was the officer who met General Lee on the road and brought him to the McLean House. While no photographs were taken of the solemn occasion, Babcock is reported to have stood on Lee's right. It is possible that this presentation sword from his brother was with Orville. (AC)

Inscription on Babcock's Sword. This sword from Ames Manufacturing was given to Babcock in February 1863. He probably had it with him in Knoxville when he arrived later in the fall. Strangely, the sword itself seems to be of French manufacture, etched and engraved by Ames; research is still underway. (AC)

JOHN WATKINS'S ARTILLERISTS JACKET. Cpl. John Watkins was an eyewitness to the Battle of Fort Sanders. An Ohio artillerist, his letters home detailed the horror of the day. He later revisited Knoxville for the Blue and Gray Reunions in 1890 and 1895, describing how deteriorated the fortifications were. (MM)

OLD GRAY CEMETERY. Established in 1850, this is the final resting place of so many Knoxvillians with poignant Civil War stories. Civilians and soldiers, Confederate and Unionist, the people who had permission to kill each for four long years of war now lie side by side in lasting peace in this beautiful East Tennessee outdoor art gallery. (MM)

ARCHAEOLOGY AT FORT HIGLEY. Though recently threatened with destruction, this pristine fort on the south side of the river has survived to the present almost untouched. It has now been purchased and preserved by the Aslan Foundation and will be open to the public. The almost unknown Battle of Armstrong Hill was fought at the base of the knob on which this fort sits. (AC)

ARCHAEOLOGY AT A CONFEDERATE BATTERY. The only known Confederate battery physically located in Knoxville was excavated in 2009. The trench, gun emplacement, caisson wheel ruts, and carbon-firing residue were all discovered. Minie balls, belt buckles, Edgefield pottery, nails, and knapsack hardware all escaped prior discovery by untrained people manning metal detectors. The site is now partially preserved in the midst of sorority-house construction on the University of Tennessee campus. (Courtesy of Archaeological Research Lab, University of Tennessee.)

Barbara Blount Hall on the Hill. Every town has its ghost stories, and the site of the old Barbara Blount Hall at the University of Tennessee is one. When the ground was excavated for the construction of the building in the early 1900s, the graves of Civil War dead were discovered. Though the remains were removed, undergraduates like to scare themselves with stories of multiple sightings of ghostly uniformed soldiers drilling on the hilltop. (SPCL)

Monument to Admiral Farragut. In 2010 this fine statue of David Glasgow Farragut was erected in the town named in his honor. The actual cannon from his ship was acquired and made a permanent part of the memorial. Engraved stones around the garden tell the story of his long and successful naval career. (AC)

Adm. David Glasgow Farragut. This famous Civil War hero was born west of Knoxville beside the Tennessee River, where his father operated a ferry. While he left the area as a child, his birthplace is recognized, and a town was named in his honor. Recently, at the Farragut Town Hall, a fine statue was erected, and a cannon from his ship was installed as a memorial to his service in the US Navy. (LC)

Consistent with our mission to preserve history on a local level, this book was printed in South Carolina on American-made paper and manufactured entirely in the United States. Products carrying the accredited Forest Stewardship Council (FSC) label are printed on 100 percent FSC-certified paper.

MADE IN THE USA